I0123346

Be A Man

Edited by Joseph Phillips

Cover design by David Gagne

©2013, Big Owl Publishing, LLC

Big Owl Publishers, LLC

editor@bigowlpublishing.com

Sarasota, FL 34236

www.bigowlpublishing.com

Forward

My hair has receded. My knees hurt in the morning. There's a little paunch around my waist. My once-blond beard has some clumps of gray and there are lines around my eyes. I can't do the all-nighters, even the late-nighters, like I used to. I'm old and, hopefully getting older. No, I'm not an ancient dinosaur, but I'm getting there.

As I look back on my life I think of all the older men who've steered my right and wrong: my dad, my uncles, brothers, pastors, teachers, and bosses. Some of the advice I've embraced, while other advice I've foolishly thrown back like too-small fish. If only I'd learned that these were nuggets of wisdom that my elders were freely giving to me, how much better my life today would be. And how better of a man I would be now.

So that's what's in this book. I've asked men that I admire if they'd share the wisdom of their mistakes, the gems from their experiences, and the advice they wish they'd known long ago. Some of the guys in here are nearly twice my age and some of the men are a few years younger than me. The men in this book have been constant friends, advisors, counselors, drinking buddies, fellow philosophers, but always men of character.

I hope you listen to what they have to say. I hope you apply what you can learn herein. I hope you live an exciting, adventurous, smart, and long life.

Joseph Phillips, Editor

Table of Contents

Male Identity: The Unique Male Essence

By Jonathan Acosta

My kindergarten report card had a section toward the bottom of the back flap with the following words: "Jonathan lacks self-confidence."

I don't recall seeing it as a small child but later I felt rubbed raw about that assessment having been etched into my personal history. I never memorized any other mark on that report card.

Such critiques breed self-awareness however; and as I grew up, that mark helped me gauge the strength of my internal stability as well as my connections to, and involvement in, the events around me. This and the positive male roles played by a hard-working father and four older brothers, coupled with the sensitivity of a loving mother, endowed me with self-confidence and what I consider a strong, healthy definition of what it means to be a man.

In my youth, all the tenets of masculinity and male identity I possessed more or less matched those I witnessed in the world around me; in society, in the media, among friends and even strangers. It never came into question nor was it ever challenged or attacked by those around me.

As I have grown older, however, I have not only noticed a slow but progressive erosion in the number of men that reach what I consider foundational basics in stable and healthy male identity, but I have also witnessed an almost staggering increase in the way men and the male identity are attacked in the world.

Men in World View

In the wake of these changes, I have often felt compelled to address how the world now views men and I am convinced that the coming generations of young men will be in dire need of traditional reference and perspective. Sadly, there was once a time when women suffered great repression and derision in a world that was considered the exclusive realm of men. It's equally sad that in many respects the pendulum has now swung.

When I began to collect my thoughts on the subject of male identity, it became evident that *many* of the terms I often thought sufficiently addressed the male identity were equally important in defining female identity.

So I have, to the best of my ability, narrowed the following points down to those that experience has taught me are indispensable to the healthy self-recognition and shaping of the male identity.

Confidence. I can scarcely think of a word more pivotal to the foundation and day-to-day function of a man. I once heard a fellow Marine speak exclusively on its importance but initially shrugged it off as proud and overstated until I came to realize that every function, every endeavor, ever first step we take as men begins with a moment of concrete self-confidence. And the moment it is lacking we can falter or fail. In hindsight, it is no wonder to me now that this Marine attained the rank of sergeant and became a respected leader among his men for he constantly displayed an internal stability, calm, and forthright nature borne of confidence in his regular interactions with them, even in the manner with which he carried himself. Close fraternal orders such as the Marine Corps imbues each member with an alpha-male persona steeped in self-confidence and with that persona comes new potential for accomplishment.

Through a similar bonding interaction, a father is able to transfer a seed of his own confidence to his son. Although this inculcation of confidence and initial shaping of depth in a young man is the product of nurturing, it is predicated upon a natural male predisposition for two exceptional abilities; to incorporate confidence from external male role models and to reflect and manifest this input externally.

It is through this state of self-confidence that another critical male virtue is brought to bear: courage. To some degree, courage and self-confidence are interchangeable: courage is an acute *state* of self-confidence and is best measured in the presence of fear. Every man experiences fear and this is perfectly acceptable. The idea of a man who is fearless in the face of danger is an unrealistic concept and more a figure of speech than reality. A man who lacks fear in the face of a trying challenge is either not mature enough or simply too foolish to appreciate its gravity.

Yet, it is not success or failure that should affirm our courage; it is the handling of our fear in the face of possible failure, ridicule, or danger that defines it. Courage leads us to act in spite of fear; and through action, we accomplish. Consequently, the likelihood of success tends to rise in direct proportion to challenges that are approached with genuine self-confidence.

The critical role of this virtue is not limited to exceptional challenges, however. It plays a role in all of our social interactions; our split-second decisions at school, work, or on the road and even in the seemingly mundane goals we take on throughout the day.

Men and Women

In delving deeper into the male identity, it is important to make a few comparisons and distinctions between how men and women function. What is it about the internal male framework that causes us to stand apart? Well-known minister and marriage counselor Mark Grungor sums it up best when he describes the male brain as functioning by way of individual compartments, addressing each in a singular manner with energies focused on one compartment at a time without requiring emotional connections to other compartments;

whereas women are primarily designed to internally address a multitude of emotionally interconnected compartments at any given time.

Although this ability to "detach" from synergistic thought and emotion often characterizes men as insensitive or brutish, it is precisely this ability that defines much of our proper function in world. Mature and objective men and women learn to view these two processes as simply distinct approaches without mistakenly assigning either as superior.'

It is important to note that although it is not an absolute necessity for men to develop enhanced physical strength to define ourselves or to succeed in life, in general it is undeniable that we are endowed with a definite edge over woman in such areas and the development of one's physique goes beyond the superficial. For men, the development of strength and physical prowess touches upon predatory, primal roots that remain hard-wired in the human male. Putting aside for a moment the simplified end-role that physical attraction plays between the sexes, physical strength informs a man's concept of self and place in society.

Physical strength is connected to confidence and courage. We relate more readily to the hunter, to the warrior, to the adrenaline-pumped aggression and love for technical complexity that drives many of our interests and pursuits as men. We not only tend to favor the fishing rod and the axe, the hammer and the spear, we even experience inexplicable pangs for their use. In modern times, we fill the void with a rifle, an engine, a truck, or a power tool, and a hardy physique complements their use and enhances the man's connection to his deeply ingrained self-image.

Our natural potential for enhanced physical strength, combined with our 'singularized' thought processes enable us shoulder the most trying of circumstances, unhindered, which leads to another unique trait: stamina. As men we are the bearers of brunt. This physical resilience tends to carry into emotional resistances as well. Thus we are called upon to endure, through physical and emotional trials. We are expected to resist, to weather, to shrug off pain and fatigue. We take pride in being immovable in the face of adversity so that those we protect, those who may not be as well equipped to resist, may survive and flourish in their own strengths. Consequently, we are often looked to and depended upon to fill certain social expectations.

The Traditional Male Role

In defining the male identity and ourselves as men, we have broken down part of the internal male construct; but what of our 'external place in the world? How does his internal structure translate into external connectivity?

Take a moment to consider the handful of particular internal attributes mentioned above: confidence and courage, singular thought, strength, physical prowess, and resilience. With few exceptions, this combination of internal traits occurs almost exclusively among men. It should come as no surprise then that across all cultures, societies and disciplines, men are so consistently self-driven and called upon to fill roles of leadership. Although not absolute, with enough maturity and experience, we are often able to tackle the dynamics of such roles with ease.

Our self-confidence helps us make decisions and once made, it keeps us from over-thinking and questioning those decisions. Our emotional focus and our resilience allow us to see our endeavors through and help us to demonstrate success to others in the face of adversity. The combination of these effects assures others that we are indeed worthy of respect and trust. This is the core essence of a man's leadership ability: the measure of his 'worthiness.'

What is the value of leadership? Since the dawn of civilization, men heave filled virtually all critical leadership roles in their respective cultures and societies. Sure, dominant physical strength secured our 'place' since the moment the first man and woman set their eyes on each other. Taking charge of a situation has always come naturally to us. We are doers and go-getters. We revel in being at the front and take pride in having others look up to us and follow. It is not just in our blood. Even in modern times, where the lines that once defined the roles and responsibilities of the sexes have become blurred, our innate male nature still wants to return to its roots, to the alpha-wolf buried deep in our X-Y chromosome.

But with that dominant strength came other responsibilities. We were called upon to be the protectors, the providers, and the laborers upon whose shoulders fell the most backbreaking work that needed doing. Finally, and this point cannot be overemphasized; we are the lovers of women. Our fascination and our drive to captivate, cherish, and lift up our beautiful female counterparts is central to our identity as men.

As a result, the roles best suited and most required of men were those of husband and father, which have ensured the safety and proliferation of succeeding generations and the passing down of critical traits such as confidence, stability, and leadership to his male and female offspring.

The Male Role in Modern Society

There are those who claim that the traditional male role is under threat of extinction in modern society and the common existential view that no one has the right to define what makes someone a man is an obstacle against enlightenment and any return to our previous, healthy understanding of masculinity. I agree that the boundaries of manhood cannot and *should* not be relegated to some contrived, infinitesimal set of details. But it is perfectly plausible that there are some fundamental parameters that should be imparted to every man, just as there are fundamental parameters in the making of a good parent, a good officer, a good servant, and etcetera.

From my late teen years throughout my twenties, I noticed a subtle shift in attitude toward men in American culture. I noticed increasing occurrences of passive animosity toward the male gender in entertainment, especially television. Films, scripted dramas, and sitcoms didn't concern me too much because one accepted those characters and situations as creative license, even though their plots exuded a considerable degree of inherent animosity toward men. The commercials were what I found particularly irksome. I noticed it became increasingly popular for male characters to be portrayed as blunder some, fault-worthy sideline spectators who tended to be on the losing side of encounters with women more often than not. In my young mind at the time, these breaks between scheduled programming provided a fantasy relief and a supposed glimpse into a reality I was supposed to relate to and accept, whether or not the ulterior motive was the sponsor's interest in selling a product. Fortunately, I was somehow able to pick up on something feeling out of place among this growing anti-male sentiment in entertainment. I remember at a very young age feeling the need to champion what I witnessed becoming one of the most vilified groups in western society. Today, the bulk of advertisement revels in this fictitious situational dominance of men by women and much of society has been erringly convinced.

The problem is that such sensory input on a mass scale is socially impactful and begins to modify general attitude over time. Nowadays, it is commonplace to view male bashing as a benign event, without expectation of any controversy or backlash. In most any social circle, the suggestion of kicking a man in the groin or the severing his penis are considered sources of humor in spite of the horrific nature of either act. The insidious, circular mechanisms that enable this social condition are the passive but aggressively-replicated concepts that, *men can take it* and *woe to any man who speaks out in objection for he is less of a man to do so.*

To a certain extent, there is some merit to this concept. The male physique and psyche have natural predispositions for strength, resistance and stoicism and an individual man can indeed find security in coming to terms with these internal predispositions and their bulwark effects against personal attacks. But in the environment that surrounds him in the so-called progressive perspective of western society, men are expected to remain silent; persistently self-effaced victims of the very virtues endowed upon them by their gender.

The real damage to a society rising from this erosion of respect toward men manifests itself in subtle ways and in the long term. With each successive generation, boys are progressively exposed to the false concept of being inferior to girls. Consistently, a boy's naturally hard-wired male virtues come into collision with the increasingly weakened male nurturing portion of his evolution into manhood, that which is normally available through his exposure to strong male role models. Degrading into a perpetual cycle, we breed weaker men and weaker male role models to guide them, consecutively bred in environments that are progressively derisive toward the male gender.

This weakness is evident in the increasing proliferation of young men afraid to be aggressive, afraid to confront challenges, afraid to speak up in groups, afraid to lead, afraid even to show their masculinity, the last being most undermining. One need only look to the recent past to see evidence of this regress. Exceptional cases aside, the daring, indomitable fighting men of two world wars were not given to weak tones or small feats, nor given to broad-stroked emasculation of any sort, not at their own hands nor at the hands of others. In fact, what defined men and women in the first half of the twentieth century was a well-defined propriety distinct to each gender.

There existed what one might consider a collective socio-emotional interconnectivity between men and women, one that was mutually complimentary and engendered a certain respect and a well-defined distinction between the sexes and each one's uniqueness in the world. These were times when chivalry was not marred by negative connotation. The suggestion that paramount among male roles was the protection and support of women could be made without ascribing women with a character of subservience or weakness or one of superiority or dominance over men.

In the long wake of the well-intended movement of Women's Suffrage at the turn of the 20th century, the so-called 'revolutionary' social movements of the 1960's and 70's marked an overt blurring of these distinctions and the defining strengths and particular roles of both genders. This laid the foundation for modern forms of "acceptable" emasculation of men in our culture. The Suffrage Movement of the United States helped secure voting rights for American women and led to provisions for equal opportunity in the workforce, two considerations that became necessary to preserve basic, social respect for women in a rapidly advancing world. Once these legal measures were in place however, the movement's inertia became somewhat of a socio-psychological runaway train after the 1950's, carrying with it poorly-secured resentments toward men, finally jumping the tracks of human rights, wrecking the necessary divide between the sexes and undermining the valuing of men and masculinity.

In the process, western society has moved toward a collective state of oversensitivity. We have developed an underdog mentality; one that jumps at any instance that might remotely feel like defense of the weak, even at the cost of upholding what is morally just. We now excuse weakness in people as a choice, a manner that cannot, that *should* not be helped. We look upon those who are indecisive, indifferent, and immoral by choice as victimized and any reprimand of such faults by a person of strength, stability, wisdom, or proven experience easily becomes prey to misplaced, overt political correctness by those who feel it their calling to rescue the assaulted. The word *masculine* has taken on a negative connotation and is used as a derisive adjective.

In recent years, coupled with the increasingly popular liberal idea that we should be allowed to do whatever we want without fear of consequence, this deterioration has taken Western society into one of its most sickened states. We have seen our tolerance for homosexuality, once seen as a deviance from sexual morality and social moorings, to the embracement of it. In fact, nowadays, homosexuality is seen by the liberal mind as something that can do no harm but is simply another state of being. This uplifting of damaged men and the repression of male heterosexuality now has us in a crippled gender spiral.

Unfortunately, it is often women who spearhead the defense of soft men and antagonize heterosexual men. Unwittingly, these women become the victims of their own devaluation of stable men. In the process of deriding straight men in society, they help produce a degraded availability of the very masculine men so many of them are naturally, exclusively attracted to.

One of the most insecure behaviors I witness regularly today is the wrathful vitriol of alleged "progressives" claiming to be free of gender-bias who, ironically, recoil, writhe, and foam at the mouth the moment a man makes any modest attempt to define manhood, masculinity, or maleness. To these individuals, it is impossible for a man to humbly seek definition or understanding about his manhood, educate his kid on male identity, or help a young male adult find the man in himself, without being viewed as insecure and wanting to punch homosexuals and chain what must be his gagged and perpetually pregnant woman to the kitchen stove. For if a man dares to discuss manhood or, God forbid, find any praiseworthy strength in his 'maleness' or stability in his heterosexuality, he must want to oppress the world!

An Experience in Extremes

It is only now in my late thirties that I have come to realize how unique my set of experiences has truly been. Aside from the fortune of having come from a stable family, my parents having remained married to old age, I took it upon myself to recover some of time I had wasted in my twenties and at age 33, I took a drastic step to counter the onset of an impending midlife crisis and enlisted in the United States Marine Corps. In all honesty, I did not make the decision out of some sense of patriotic duty. I did it for the selfish purpose of improving myself. I enlisted because I wanted to become a better man and I knew this extreme commitment would transform my self-confidence as well as imbue me with a unique self-discipline that would impact all areas of my life in the coming years.

During my time in this exclusive organization, I worked closely with some of the most aggressive, alpha males one could meet. While undergoing basic training on Parris Island however, I noticed a wide variety of personalities among the aggressive recruits, many from different parts of the United States and a few from places as far as Thailand and Liberia. Each of them came from disparate upbringings and possessed different sets of skills as well as varying internal strengths and weaknesses. Some were innocent and immature, having never been away from their parents before, some were well educated and serious minded and of course, there were those young men who fit the ideal killer-in-training profile; empty of mind, cold, and open to indoctrination. In those first six months between Parris Island and Camp LeJeune, we all received the same massive dose of training in the professional dispensation of violence.

Basic training was physically and mentally gut-wrenching. One might describe it as constant controlled trauma. Among the many unforgettable experiences on the Island that broke me down and remade me as a man, one of them marked a particularly memorable moment of self-discovery. At the time, I was spending the days being trained on how to kill. This training covered the gamut of destructive behavior; from hand-to-hand combat to the operation of a variety of weapons; from running full-speed while spear-thrusting the end of a pugil stick into another recruit's face, to driving a razor sharp bayonet into a rubber dummy's head and chest repeatedly with a primal scream that was supposed to communicate ecstatic pleasure in the ears of observing instructors. Always under the scrutiny of their oversight and brutality, I learned to do these things well. If there is anything on Parris Island that wins respect, it is violent aggressiveness.

As the typical day began to wind down toward evening and platoons of recruits retreated to their respective squad bays, we would eventually be gathered together and sat down on the floor in orderly ranks, each of us eager to receive the day's mail from loved ones, personally handed out by the Senior Drill Instructor. This was one of our few moments of respite from the day's pain. Each Senior Drill Instructor, or SDI for short, would oversee the training of his platoon for its entire "cycle" on Parris Island. Although he was sometimes as brutal in our physical training as his subordinate drill instructors, known as DI's or Kill Hats, he was also charged with the task of ensuring the well-being of his platoon, and to serve as chief role model for recruits to imitate. As part of this leadership, the SDI made sure to dole out a certain amount of camaraderie with his recruits. Occasionally, a mock set of circumstances was contrived where the SDI would suddenly show up in the middle of some particularly brutal 'training' at the hands of the Kill Hats and 'save' us from them. In our mental and physical conditions, we naively fell for the ruse every time. Virtually starved of any other social 'warmth' and instead exposed to nothing but minute-to-minute berating and punishment week after week, it is easy to understand why each platoon's SDI would come to be looked up to as its "daddy" by the recruits.

During one of these sit-down mail sessions, the SDI was addressing us while passing out mail. It was common for him to poke a little fun now and then at individual recruits during mail call, all in good humor. On this particular occasion, it was my turn. He read the name on the envelope.

"Acosta","" he said in a gritty, monotonous tone, freezing for a moment with letter in hand, staring at me through narrow eyes and with feigned disgust while letting out a long grunt and drawing subdued smiles from all of us.

He paused for a moment gently fanning the letter and to my shock suddenly turned to the rest of the platoon and calmly said, "You see you folks gotta understand...Acosta...he's more of a lover than a fighter."

I froze. It was the strangest of moments. He had uttered the words without any trace of a mocking tone but instead bordering on esteem, a tone that almost seemed to urge the rest of the platoon to respect where I was coming from. Even years later, I struggled to figure out why he had singled me out in that manner, critical, but respectful. But at that moment, I felt uneasy; uncertain as to the impact it would have on my reputation amongst the men. This was a place that prided itself on training killers and having by then shed all remnants of conscientious objection to wartime killing, I had truly become an instrument capable of delivering the intended product.

Throughout my training, I felt I had more than matched my fellow recruits in their aggressive tackling of challenges, scoring shorter running times than some of those who were up to ten years younger than me, even scoring the highest in rifle marksmanship of all 55 in my platoon and scoring second place in a company of 212 recruits.

So what was it about my being that had come across as so docile to our "daddy?" To this date, the only unusual behavior I remember exuding being the oldest member of my company was that I was the only one constantly engaged in offering spiritual support to some of the recruits during their faltering moments or when showing signs of mental wear. It was a fatherly instinct that would come out of me and was undoubtedly evident in my overall demeanor.

By the last phase of basic training, it had earned me a noticeable respect from these young men, in addition to the fact that I had kept up with them through the pain and suffering we endured together. In the wide, hellish, black-and-white scheme of Parris Island however, empathy simply had to be publicly classified as weakness for the sake of maintaining the brutal image of our purpose. But unlike my more youthful counterparts, I knew myself better and I was secure in the man I had become prior to my enlistment and secure in the role I was now playing among these young men. I had discovered how hard a warrior I could be but I was also at peace with being viewed as a 'soft' Marine.

This newly identified dichotomy in me helped me understand what I would come to view as a unique dynamic in my male identity. The important sensitivities imbued by my mother had only subconsciously deferred to the critical foundations secured in me by my father and the other male role models in my life. But this new, hard-earned dynamic would soon be tested, as I was about to enter an arena where the moorings of male identity, and practically all things masculine, would be turned on their heads.

Art School

Two years after my initial training and well into my reserve contract, I enrolled in a very prominent art school in hope of pursuing a civilian career based on an artistic talent I had developed since childhood. I had just survived one of the most physically and mentally rigorous training programs in existence and had experienced what might be considered by many as a complete overhaul and upgrade of internal confidence and self-discipline at the hands of one of the world's most elite fighting forces. I felt confident that any group I would work with would receive me with positive, high expectation. I had hoped that I might even be look up to as a Marine. But what awaited me at this art school was the absolute opposite. It was difficult enough to come from a weekend of drill duty at a military station where Marines carried out enormous, often dangerous, daily tasks with the perfect discipline and efficiency of a well-oiled machine to that of a classroom environment where the typical male student would walk in late, unkempt, unbathed, unprepared, and dressed in what was often borderline effeminate attire and accompanied by some of the most indifferent, unconfident and lackadaisical attitudes I had ever witnessed. At times, I was so disgusted by the piss-poor attitude that it was hard to suppress my desire to reach across the table and throttle what many in the world of real men would consider some of the worst excuses for young males. In short, what I learned over the four years that I pursued my bachelor's degree was that the world of the arts is saturated with liberal ideals and has no tolerance for strong male leadership or character, let alone any individual that shows any sense of male pride.

In fact, the frequency of social ostracism, derision, and verbal attacks I experienced in response to any attempt at showing a male strength of character, confidence or leadership had, by my sophomore year, caused me to shy away from all active sharing of my title as a Marine. Often treated by students, and on occasion by staff, as some overly aggressive brute, I had all but been told that it was something to be ashamed of.

Ironically, in their eyes, the "soft Marine" wasn't soft enough. I had graduated from Parris Island with a better understanding of the best of men but I had graduated from art school with a newfound disgust for my fellow man. I was thankful that in the end that I had gained invaluable perspective from witnessing the best and the worst of male identity in the world.

Your Male Identity

So, who are you as a young man? What male character do you see yourself identifying with? What male strengths do you see in your internal self? How do you see that man fitting into the outside world? As a young man, you are designed to be the pinnacle of confidence and strength in society. You are the driving force behind all accomplishment in the world and you have the opportunity to take advantage of a wealth that comes with simply being born a man. Take pride in the identity that is yours. You are hard-wired from birth to lead, to overcome obstacles and adversity and to dominate any situations or challenge. This ability is not something you have to earn. No. It is yours. It became yours the moment the powers-that-be decided that you were to receive the XY chromosome. Know that. Own that piece of information and the world will be at your fingertips.

Jonathan grew up in culturally-diverse Miami amidst the burgeoning 1980's entertainment era. The son of Christian ministers and youngest of five, he recalls a bare foot, wild-child adolescence full of innocent wonder and a fascination for the complex details of nature. He has worked for the U.S. Postal Service, served in the United States Marine Corps and has traveled Europe, the Caribbean, and South America. Having attained a BFA from Ringling College of Art & Design, Jonathan is a professional illustrator with a passion for both the animated film and video game industries. In addition to his pursuits in the realm of art and entertainment, he aspires to also work with children and in counseling teens and young adults.

On Life and Onward

By Marvin L.C. Hoffman

This I can assure you: You will look back on your life and wish you had done things differently, done different things, and not done some things.

As a man in his mid-life, I have all three misgivings; please don't misunderstand me, I have done some great things, and a great many things that I would not change for the world. For instance, although I am divorced from the mother of my children, I would not change that circumstance for anything. Not only did I gain two wonderful children, but discounting the unhappiness of a marriage unraveled, most of our marriage was happy, and she and I remain friends. Another thing is that though it could have changed the entire course of my life, I do wish I had finished college. Not just so it can be part of my resume, but rather for the feeling of accomplishment a success such as this gives to a person. Not only this success, but I know that if I had finished college, I would have a greater knowledge of the world around me; I have come to realize that knowledge is a valuable resource.

There are situations in my life that I wish I'd handled differently, hurtful things I wish I'd not said, and comforting, uplifting things I wish I had said. There are loved ones who have passed on that I wish I had spent more time with, had spoken with more, and had told them "I love you" more often. As I look back on my life, I can see so many things that could have been handled better, but to be honest, it is this collection of successes, failures, and omissions that have made me who I am today.

I'm going to share with you some important thoughts and ideas that I have to come to understand to be of greater importance; things that I realized upon closer inspection: things I feel I've done well, things I wish I hadn't done, or had done differently. Sound familiar? I have through reading and by surrounding myself with good friends and people I admire, accomplished, to a degree, that which I am sharing with you. I have tried my best to not fill this essay with hyperbole, nor with admonitions that I have not considered personally. The impetus is on you now; you will need to read and see how these apply to your life.

If some of the things I have written feel right to you and you can make them your own, perhaps the number, and the intensity of things you will reflect upon with disappointment will be minimized, and success in your life will come with less of a cost. In the end, the things you do in life, the decisions you make, even when following the best of advice, are still just past decisions with the information at hand. And even with the best consideration, and deliberation, you will still make decisions that you will rue. This is the stuff that makes up life.

Life is fluid, so whether you approach the situation of life from a scientific or spiritual perspective, one thing quickly becomes evident. The circumstances of our perception of life are very fluid; as W. B. Yeats wrote: "Things fall apart; the centre cannot hold."

This quotation, taken from *The Second Coming,* was written in the aftermath of World War I, a war to end all wars; a war which, as we know, did not end all wars.

Also the great Alfred Einstein said: "Life is like riding a bicycle. To keep your balance, you must keep moving."

Nothing in this entire universe, in all the heavens spread across the tapestry of the cosmos, is static. Nothing is unmoving, nor should the core of our being be static. Living with motion is something that has been difficult for me, even as I sit and type this, I feel stationary, but it is certain that life around me, and including me, are moving. Sometimes this can make one feel out of control, but such is the nature of life.

Using the analogy of a boatman, or the sailor at the tiller, you set a course with a destination in mind; but during the voyage you will need to steer around obstacles, you may need to avoid certain areas, and you may even need to *beat to windward*. To beat to windward in nautical terms is altering your course and the set of your sails to use a wind that is coming toward you for your best advantage. No ship can sail northward in a wind coming from the north, so an alternating from northeastward to northwestward will be used. In the short term, your course may not intuitively appear to be still set for your destination, but the competent sailor knows that he or she is still making progress, and will arrive.

Life and all its circumstances are constantly in motion; therefore there will be times when these circumstances may be contrary to the course you have set. This is where consideration comes in; consider the decisions you made when setting both your ultimate course, and your temporary course. Also don't be so set with your opinions that you cannot avoid the rocks simply because you are too stubborn to see how to avoid them.

Benjamin Franklin, from his closing speech at the Constitutional Convention of 1787 said, "For having lived long, I have experienced many instances of being obliged, by better information or fuller consideration, to change opinions, even on important subjects, which I once thought right but found to be otherwise."

From youth to a certain age my perspectives, opinions, and even beliefs have changed. Some of these have changed quite drastically; things I had been so sure of turned out to be quite iffy, while things that I thought never mattered are now quite important to me. When I was younger, I thought I had a great many things figured out. In retrospect I realize that could not be farther from the truth. Now, I feel I do have a great many things figured out. Imagine what I'll think in thirty years; most likely I'll look back and laugh at how silly I was in my fifties.

The Pulitzer Prize-winning journalist Katherine Anne Porter said: "I don't believe in intuition. When you get sudden flashes of perception, it is just the brain working faster than usual. But you've been getting ready to know it for a long time, and when it comes, you feel you've known it always."

Life is what we perceive, and the most common thing about life that changes is the amount of knowledge that we have gained throughout our lives. The circumstances of our existence, the common experiences we all receive (if we are open and receptive to them) help to shape and guide us.

It is interesting to note that the concept of the telephone was patented, independently, by two different men on the same day. Alexander Graham Bell, the man remembered as the father of the telephone, patented his conception of the telephone the same day as Elisha Gray filed a caveat to a patent. This great advancement in communication came about independently in such a close time-frame because it was time for this sort of advancement. The telegraph was already in use, and it would only be obvious that, as humans who prefer to communicate vocally rather than by tapping, this sort of advancement would be intuitive.

As we live, and as we, collectively, gather information, naturally our beliefs and opinions should evolve. Before the knowledge of germs, disease was 'obviously' the result of demons or evil spirits, but with just a tiny bit of information our understanding and beliefs change to more correctly reflect the world around us.

When I was a young man, especially growing up in East Tennessee, I was ignorant of a good many things. My views of the world were constrained to what I knew and understood. Alternative lifestyles, opinions differing from those of my immediate surroundings, family and friends, were unknown to me. Since this time my views have changed, in my opinion for the better, because of an expanded world view.

When I travel to other parts of the country, not just other parts of the world, I try to absorb what is around me. I try not to interpret the people and places solely on my current level of understanding, which would probably yield mistranslations, and misunderstandings, rather I want to accept those around me for who they are. For example, when I was a young man I would make fun of pointy-toed cowboy boots. Having grown up on the East Coast, I thought they looked silly, and anyone who wore them was a dime store cowboy. But in my mid-twenties, I lived in Idaho for a few years. I embraced the outdoor lifestyle, and at one point had a girlfriend whose parents owned a ranch. She and I would ride horses and I was invited to go on round ups. Wisely I was not allowed to have a rope. So, I bought a pair of pointy-toed cowboy boots. The boots hadn't changed, only my perception of them.

On Setting and Change Direction

Harkening back to the sailor analogy, the wise and wary sailor does not judge his entire voyage based on the conditions in the harbor; rather he continually assesses the sea and makes course corrections, perhaps beats to the wind, and other adjustments. He sees what is around him using all his senses, and responds, adapts, to make his way to his destination. You should also respond and adapt to what life gives you; keep in mind your goals, dreams, and aspirations, read the winds and sea and make adjustments to yourself and your environment appropriately, all while not violating the integrity of your morals and precepts that you use to govern your life.

Not to negate the sailor's course, but sometimes we don't have a clear destination in mind; Like some legendary sailors who set sail for points unknown, for locations that were merely ideas, guesses, and hoped for passages; our journey in life is readily apparent that it is the journey, not the destination, that is of greatest importance.

Christopher Columbus said, "Following the light of the sun, we left the Old World," and "For the execution of the voyage to the Indies, I did not make use of intelligence, mathematics or maps."

Columbus had an idea of a destination, and was discovering through journey the means to achieve this destination and with it his goals and ambitions.

We are in the same boat in our life. I'm sure you've heard the phrase, "I had to wrap my head around it," meaning, for the purpose of this essay at least, that it is so difficult for us to completely envision the penultimate conclusion of even the simplest planned adventure. Some of my greatest experiences have come not in the end game, but rather during the build up to it.

My time in the Navy is a perfect example, I had a general idea of what would happen; I would enlist, and be on a ship and have all sorts of adventures. The adventures, but most importantly the paths to these adventures were monumental moments in my life. And as it turned out, there really was no destination, only a course that was set.

Even having said all this, it is almost impossible to specifically point out things that you should, or should not do; especially considering that it's your journey that is of the most importance. And yet I can certainly recall more than one seemingly bad decision that has led me to a place of much greater wisdom.

For me this is an affirmation that the journey works to our betterment at times. You may ask what makes me think that I have the right to tell anyone how to live his or her life. You are right to ask and I say keep that questioning attitude, but remember I'm not telling anyone what to do; giving advice is not issuing an order. You can heed or ignore any and all advice, but I, like the other essay authors in this compendium, have accrued quite a few person-years of experience, and maybe, just maybe we might have some perspective. As for me, my life has been a curious and strange adventure. I was actually born in a log cabin in East Tennessee in 1960, yet later in life was a nuclear plant operator on Navy submarine. So like a line in a song, "What a long strange trip it's been."

I didn't always have guidance on how or what to do in life. My dad wasn't the most talkative type. However, he was an important figure in my life and I would hang on the stories that he would tell of his adventures in the Navy during

World War II. This was during the '60s and '70s where war movies and shows on television were quite prominent. So here I was a young man with a head packed full of the 'romantic' vision of the military, but not a lot of other guidance.

When I was seventeen my dad died tragically; this was quite the traumatic event for me. But I hold no distinction for tragedy, many men and women have lived without fathers and mothers, or worse, had abusive ones; either physical or mental. But as a young man I was in the world with a chip firmly, yet precariously balanced on my shoulder. Not long after my dad's death I started college. Now while in high school, I was just smart enough to get by with B's and C's without ever taking a book home. But sadly I was not smart enough to be able to slide through college, and I had never had to study before, so I had no study skills.

It was in my social life in college where I excelled. I had one friend, who was in the same sort of situation as me, and he and I would drink cheap wine in my dorm room and I would regale him with stories from my dad's time in the war. One night he and I decided that we would just run off and join the Navy. Though we had both made our minds up to go, on the morning we were to head to Memphis and actually swear in, I chickened out. But my friend followed through; only a few weeks later I left college and moved back home to do I don't know what.

The first thing I did was get a job at a zinc die-casting and manufacturing plant working second shift. This was a fine job, but it didn't take me long to realize that it wasn't a job for me. We would routinely take breaks, and during this time I thought it was very adult to carry liquor in my truck with me. I was nipping at a bottle of vodka when an older coworker came up and asked for a drink.

"Sure" I said, and to my amazement he turned the bottle up and drank easily a quarter of the bottle.

In that instant I saw the next 20 years of my life slip out of that bottle and down his throat. He was me; or rather the man that I would become; a sobering thought.

It was only a short time later that my mom woke me in the morning whispering, "It's long distance."

Long distance phone calls in those days were a very big thing. I answered the phone and it was my friend from college.

"Hey, Marv"," he said. "Guess where I'm calling you from?"

"Uh I don't know"," I stammered.

"Scotland," he told me with a lot of enthusiasm, "and I'm on a submarine! And guess what else?" he asked and then answered before I could guess, "I'm a torpedoman's mate, just like your dad was."

Choking back the tears I somehow finished the conversation, which I admit I remember none of. But I do remember this: I left for work early that day and stopped by a Navy recruiter. It was about a week later that I was on a plane to boot camp. Not all decisions are made through complicated levels of decision making, involving listing pros and cons. Some decisions are solely based on emotions, and though not often good, are not always bad.

All of this is my perception of what life is, the things that I personally have realized to be true for me. I have looked, and continue to look, backwards at my life in order to see who and what I am; to help me make decisions, set my course from here. These reflections aren't living in the past, but reminders that I need to the best I can be for me and for the people I love.

On Living Life

"Decisions are what you have to make when the answer isn't obvious. So do all that you can to make the answer obvious." Jim Cox President, CEO Medkinetics, LLC.

Understand that your journey has already commenced and it is taking place with you within the confines of society. Society, just like life, is fluid and continually changing. Many of the things that were acceptable in my youth are very much looked down upon now. So you will have to live within the parameters that modern society has set.

First things first, avoid extremism, all things in moderation. Religion and spirituality are good things as they can help us get over many of the hardships of life, but try to avoid extreme religious groups. While I'm on this subject, my advice is to always be skeptical. Be a freethinker and make your own decisions.

Thomas Jefferson wrote: "Fix reason firmly in her seat, and call to her tribunal every fact, every opinion. Question with boldness even the existence of a

God; because, if there be one, he must more approve of the homage of reason, than that of blindfolded fear."

When I was younger, I did realize that there was a lot I didn't know and in order to have opinions, or come to conclusions I would rely on experts and people I knew who had more experience than me. This is neither right nor wrong, it's just necessity. We do need to rely on the society in which we live to help us exist. Just remember that when you talk to others, they often share with you only the facts (good and bad) that support their solidly-held beliefs. You can feel free to use this in guiding your own decisions, but make these decisions yours.

Try to understand why you believe what you do. Is it because it is from how you were raised? Extremists often use emotional judgment only, and most often ignore, or disregard out of hand, facts and evidence that contradicts what they choose to believe. This is living in ignorance, and like a wrong number placed in a square in Sudoku, will prevent you from making the best decisions later on in the game of life. Extremists by their very nature are exclusive, and because they, by definition, live in ignorance can lead to bad decisions, even dangerous decisions. Life is a very precious thing; so far life on earth as we know it is the only life in existence in the universe. To avoid extremism, be skeptical, and make your decisions. And this is paramount: understand that the beliefs that you are so sure of today may turn out to be not so certain to the smarter and wiser future you.

We human beings have evolved into very social creatures. We love to clique up and form into exclusive groups. Have you ever wondered at how we ask, "So, what are you having?" when we go to restaurants with friends? I think we all want to feel that our decisions have some corroboration. Being a freethinker doesn't mean to never take advice or to not be part of clubs, social organizations, or even religious organizations. But rather to not rely on these outside influences to make your decisions for you.

Give yourself the freedom to explore, and determine where your interests lie. Yes, have your opinions, and stick to your principles, but be open to new things. Just because something is foreign to you doesn't mean it is bad; it also doesn't mean it is good, you always have to use judgment, just be open.

On Failure and Success

This is what life is about: getting up when you fall. Don't give up when something falls through the first time, or the seventeenth time, just pick up where you are, weather the consequences, fix your plan, and continue on. Giving yourself permission to fail also applies to bad habits. When it comes time in your life to stop doing something, especially something that is difficult to shed, you will likely fail the first time you try. This is alright, if it were easy, you would probably not have to struggle to quit this thing. Just realize where you are, and reaffirm your goals and continue on.

Giving yourself permission to fail does not mean giving permission to be lazy, or to keep on with bad habits; but merely to not give up on what is worthwhile. When someone asks me if I'm a smoker, my answer is yes. In my adult life, I have been a non-smoker longer than a smoker. I know that if I were to smoke a cigarette, I stand teetering on the edge of becoming a smoker again. And If I buy a pack of cigarettes, I will be a pack a day smoker within a couple of weeks. I suppose I just have a physiological propensity for smoking. And I have smoked a cigarette or two whilst imbibing in a few drinks, but I take care to not let it get a hold on me again.

But when I was quitting, I gave myself permission to fail. If I fell off the wagon and started habitually smoking again then I would not throw my hands up in disgust and give in. No, I would merely consider it a valiant attempt and try again. Perhaps I would muster up more resolve, or maybe cut back on my drinking to help in my attempt to quit smoking, but I would not give up.

I heard a story once about a director who would always bring several ideas to the board meetings, and usually they all were realized as bad ideas. But often this director would bring pearls to the meeting, and these pearl of ideas were often parlayed into lucrative projects. This director, Ted Turner, was not afraid of failure. It may have even appeared that he embraced the failure, but through the attempts, successful and otherwise, his success evolved. Be like Ted Turner in this resolve; don't be afraid to try something because you're simply afraid to fail.

Love everyone, but trust few. Throughout your life you will, hopefully, be amidst a great torrent of new people, some will become great friends, some will remain acquaintances, but some, as they should be, will hopefully be expunged. Remember that each person you meet is truly a free moral agent = that is someone who has free will. My advice is to always have at least one good friend with whom you can talk openly and freely. The phrase "No man is an island" means that we can't exist in complete solitude. It is vital that you be your own person, as you too are a free moral agent, but you are not alone. Nor should you be.

Close friends are vital, having people you can trust and depend on will make your life's navigation much easier. When you are in social situations, be open to meeting new people, especially those with differing viewpoints. Because everyone is living his or her life according to decisions that he or she has made, realize that the interest of others will likely not be to your best interest. Don't be quick to blurt out personal or private information, and certainly never share financial or intimate details with any but those whom you know very well, and can trust.

While I advise you to be sociable, I'll also advise you to learn to be able to be alone. I don't mean become a hermit, but balance your social time with time alone with your thoughts and introspection. This is one I still have to work on. I am a very sociable person, but by my nature, I tend to want to be alone.

Work hard, regardless of your wages. This is work ethic, and will be something used to readily define you. If you aren't content with your wages then you must do something to change your situation, but this does not mean to minimize your work ethic. Even if you are in what you consider to be a worthless or dead-end job you can grow in this. Most certainly shop around for a better work situation, but apply yourself, and even in the negative surroundings do your job. Keep your word. You will learn to overcome adversity, to work amidst strife, and (in my opinion) be able to focus amidst a tempest.

With the work ethic you will develop imagine how you will flourish when you are in a supportive work environment. But when you are in that supportive work environment, remember your work ethic, do not feel that you have "arrived" and let your work ethic slip. Unless you win the lottery, you will have to work, and you will spend more time at your job than you do in most anything else in your life. Your work ethic is something that is yours that you can take with you from job to job, and is clearly the biggest thing that people will notice about you in the workplace.

On Letting Go and Holding Fast

Don't be afraid to let go, but hold on fiercely to those things which you hold dearest. As I mentioned earlier, my father died when I was a teen, and afterwards I developed a very special relationship with my mother. I suppose the realization that you can lose anything at any time, made me very sensitive to those closest to me. I found that if my mom and I had any disagreement, I would quickly come and apologize. I could not leave anything hanging between us. Through the years as I grew older, I came to a more mature relationship with my mother, and we would disagree, or have differences of opinions, but I still held a very dear relationship with her.

A couple of years ago she developed lung cancer and died. I was, of course, hurt, and I miss her terribly, but I am not dwelling on the past. I have sold the house that she left to me, and am moving on. I will continue to hold the memory of her close in my heart, but it is time to let the superficial things go. Physical things are not the most important, relationships and people are.

Avoid judgment. Try not to judge life prematurely. In a court of law, both the prosecution and defense present facts before the judge and jury. It is then up to the jury to decide if the defendant is guilty. The judge then sentences the defendant if found guilty. There are many innocent people in jail because not all the facts were presented, because the facts were corrupted or perverted in some fashion, or because of false facts presented. Likewise there are very many guilty people out on the street. The problem with judgment is that we often don't have all the facts.

During the O. J. Simpson trial, when the verdict was delivered, I recall watching a news broadcast of different groups of people awaiting the verdict. Depending on various factors, the different groups responded differently. In the aftermath of this murder trial, I've talked with many people, and a many of those people had solid opinions on the verdict.

"Well, a murderer went free"," was a common comment. But also I've heard, "A black man finally got a just judgment."

I have my own opinion, but I relate this case because this was the first time that I had an inkling about the concept of judgment in real life. I was lucky enough to realize that I did not have all the facts. Though many of the facts were related through the media, I realized that we were not always seeing everything in context. Well, at least the context that the prosecution or defense may have intended for them to be presented in. But I realized that O.J. really may have been innocent, as well as guilty. The jury deliberated, and found him not guilty. I will share that in my mind he sure seemed guilty, and in retrospect he was found guilty in a civil trial, but it was not for me to pronounce a judgment on him.

When I was in college, I met a guy who was skinny, bucktoothed, and pimply. He would talk about all the women he had had, and I was incredulous.

There's no way he could get women, I would think.

I, of course, was womanless at the time, and I suppose I could not bear to think that he could get women and I could not. So using my own emotions, I judged the situation. Then at a party once he came with two women on his arms. I had judged wrongly. My point being that in great and small matters it is best to try to collect all the facts, present them (to yourself if this is the case) and then you may feel free to make a judgment. But remember you are judging the facts, not the people. It is all too common in many religious circles to judge people when it is really their actions that you may be finding offensive.

The only rules are the laws and social conventions that we humans have put in place. You do not have to do any certain thing at any certain time. You should vote, but you don't have to. You may want to get married and have kids, but you don't have to. Over the years, societal norms have changed. Compared to the length of human existence, it has not been that long ago that marrying at twelve or thirteen was not just normal, but preferred.

The collective wisdom of we humans has grown, and hopefully will continue to grow. When I was a young man, the advice that I heard was to 'get a good job with a company, and you'll be set for life.' Looking at the state of careers now, people tend to switch jobs every few years, and advance as they go. Also, the particular companies that were mentioned to me as a young man are no longer viable choices for long standing careers. I look back now and realize that had I opted to follow this advice, I would not be in the position I am in today. I would not have been able to realize the growth of knowledge, and experience that I have. And I most like would not be writing this essay right now.

Dustin Hoffman's character in the movie *The Graduate* was advised 'plastics' for his career choice. Society tends to guide us along a collective path bounded only by haphazard events. You only have to watch reality television to see that societal rules, or norms, are often misguided at best. Here's some clear-cut advice: follow the best medical advice available, and abide by the laws of the land. But as for societal rules, merely take them as advice. Society may frown on tattoos, for instance, but perhaps a tattoo is not bad. A face full of tattoos is considered extreme, so be prepared to withstand the consequences if you were to choose that. Just don't let 'Aunt Harriet' urge you to get married just because you're already in your 30s and no kids for her to entertain. That, my friend, is for you to decide.

On Finances

Living this big world is both easy and difficult. But easy or difficult, one thing is certain: it's expensive just to live. You will need money. Money is an important thing, but not the most important thing. Money is just a tool for living in our society and you'll need to learn how to use this tool wisely.

Most folks misquote the Bible concerning money. You will hear many times, "Money is the root of all evil." This is not true. The Bible says, "The *love* of money is the root of all evil." And this could not be truer and more readily apparent. If you look around you in life, in politics, and even in religion, you will see people who are in love with money, and this trait has taken ownership of them. But, in my opinion, the most important thing about financial management is that this is one of the most basic keys to freedom in life.

If you can manage your means, and live within your means, then no one can impose a financial stranglehold on you. You won't have to stay at a job you hate because you have to have the paycheck. But, do not allow the finances to inhibit your life; live within your means but still yet—live!

Here's some honesty: finance management is my kryptonite. I can't really tell you why, but money management has always been hard for me. I am a reasonably intelligent fellow; I was a qualified nuclear plant operator on a Navy submarine but the ongoing management of money or lack thereof is difficult. Yet I don't think it has to be, as the punch line of a joke goes, "Curiosity got the best of him, so he went to the desk of the world's greatest accountant, and pulled open the drawer that he had seen him open every day of his career, and here is what he saw: *Debit on the left, credit on the right."*

Sorry if I ruined the joke for you, but this sort of lets us know that it is just minding the pennies. I could probably write a book about how to not manage your money, so know that the advice I give in this section is from direct experience.

I'm sure it sounds academic, but to manage your money, you will have to manage your money! And the root of this is to make a budget. You can't get out of this, and I can almost guarantee that your first several attempts at making and sticking to a budget will fail. I know this because mine have usually failed. I think it's because of a lack of continual care. Like a plant needs water continually to thrive, your personal finances also need care. Take to heart the personal part, as your financial means are actually an extension of yourself.

To create and maintain a budget here are some considerations: Don't reinvent the wheel, take advantage of existing resources. There are lots of computer programs to help manage your finances, I have my favorite, but it's often more than what I need. Currently I'm using a simple spreadsheet to manage my bill payment checklist, and my budget. I keep the two completely separate so that I can quickly make sure I'm up to date on paying my bills, and the other is how I can determine if I'm overspending.

Another very important piece of advice that I feel compelled to give you is that your personal finances are yours. End of statement. Not yours and your mother's. Not yours and your wife's. Yours. And it is your responsibility to yourself to manage your finances. I have failed more than once because I relinquished my financial management to someone else. And worse, I did not oversee the management, I just let it go. This would have to be the worst scenario possible. Do not let this happen to you. Know where your finances are; know what your financial standing is.

You may decide to get married someday. Congrats. But if and when you do, I would say to you to keep your finances separate. Oh sure, you may get a joint account to pay combined bills from and such, but keep your personal finances separate. Financial problems are one of the biggest factors in marital strife. Keep your finances in order, and perhaps be an example to your spouse, or potential spouse.

No matter how grand your finances are, they still need management. I honestly hope that everyone who reads this essay becomes financially successful, and that you will need an accountant to keep your finances straight. Tax consultants, investment counselors, all are helpful and perhaps necessary aides to your financial management, but it is still your finances. I have a close personal friend who has experienced great financial success in his life, but he can still tell you pretty closely as to what's in his bank account. He takes advantage of the tools around him but still balances his books in a spreadsheet. It is not the tools that manage your money, it's you.

On Decision Making

The process of decision making is probably the most vital of all the advice I can share. If I had not chosen to be at a certain place at a certain time I may not have met the mother of my children. I consider this to a monumental moment in my life; decisions, even tiny decisions, have completely altered my life.

Making decisions can almost always be looked at in the light of risk assessment. While driving, if you are at an intersection, you look at the cross traffic and make an assessment of whether you can beat that car and make it through the crossing or if the car is just too close or coming too fast. Every major decision, and even minor decisions, are ultimately really up to you; do a risk assessment. I haven't always been consciously aware of this idea, but in retrospect I believe it's true. The idea of risk is quite a variable thing; variable from person to person. For example, some of you may think that a girl with a tattoo is a risk – and maybe that's true for some and not true for others. Either way, when you meet someone with whom you may become romantically involved, don't let your hormones completely rule the situation. You should definitely use some risk assessment in the situation. When you marry someone, they and everything about them become a very intimate part of your life, as does everything about you become part of your spouse.

When you take a job, you become a part of the organization. This too can be a risk. If it turns out that that organization is committing illegal activities, even if you are not directly involved, you could be legally implicated, and certainly your job history will forever have a possible black mark. Of course, that's the worst-case scenario, but the choices you make, the people and company you keep, all carry risk that may negatively or positively affect your life for a long, long time.

A couple of years ago I went to France for a vacation. I fell in love with France, so much so that when I returned I started taking French lessons with a tutor. One day I would love to move to France, but I have to be, and am, aware that this does have risk associated with it. The European Union is going through some hard times right now, and France has an immigration problem that they are dealing with right now. Many of the immigrants are jobless and many are part of extremist groups. There have been several dangerous situations occur in France as of late. I am aware of all of these, and though I am not in a position to be able to act on my impulse of moving to France at the moment, I will continue to consider all of the risks and all of the rewards.

When the situation of my life becomes such that I could possibly relocate then I will weigh the risks and the impact the risks may bring. But, and with this example I want to say that sometimes one has to go with his heart, unless the risks significantly outweigh the benefits I would probably make the decision to go to France. Part of life is realizing the risks, but doing it anyway. It's just the consequences, the impact, that aren't so much fun. Risk in itself isn't a bad thing, it's the negative impact that we don't like so much.

Risk assessment helps you create plans, create contingencies. You must plan thoroughly, but it's okay to act impulsively. Don't be afraid to do something on the spur of the moment, some of life's greatest adventures can be derived from this. Of course I don't mean illegal activities, but opportunities to experience something you may never experience again. Don't go to France and sit in your hotel room. Life, in France or in your home town, is meant to be experienced.

Think of the future, but live today. Definitely don't live in the past, the past is complete. The future is not set, and quantum physicists currently lend credence to the theory that all outcomes are possible. Always be ready to change, accept new ideas and thoughts. When a tree becomes inflexible, even a medium wind can break it.

David Eagleman, a neuroscientist at Baylor University, discusses the limitations of the current state of artificial intelligence and says that it has missed a basic natural phenomenon. Every living creature is born with a certain knowledge, or intelligence. A newborn colt can be running within hours of its birth. How did it learn this so quickly? This knowledge was already present passed down genetically. You have built-in 'programs' running in your brain and these programs continue to get fine-tuned as you live and learn. What does this mean? Trust your gut. When something feels wrong, consider the likelihood that it just might be.

Loosely coupled with decision making is the idea of you living your life, not your life living you. In my life I often have been controlled within my decision making by external factors—for example, being behind in my bills. And it was situations such as these that dictated how I would, and could, live. Part of this is complacency, when everything is running along just fine, life was boring. So I think that subconsciously, because I had learned how to handle difficult financial times, I would subconsciously allow situations to get out of control, and thus put me in a place that was not boring and that I was comfortable with; because I had learned how to handle these situations, not because it was actually comfortable. Life was living me, not the other way around. I'm happy to say that now I am living my life, and though things are boring at times, I'm learning to live with that.

On Integrity

I have given many admonitions. I have urged you to be aware of the circumstances of life, and using a sailing analogy advised you to consider making course corrections, to consider altering your opinions, to be world aware, and try to absorb what will make you a better you. All good, all admirable, but I want to add a caveat to all of this: the you that is comprised of your experiences—the collection of events and decisions that you have taken in and owned to this point in life—affects what you do now and what you'll do later.

Your wonderful brain has taken these things and the id, the *you* that is you, has evaluated and created a set of principles that the embedded software will unconsciously use to evaluate all of the external feeds from your senses. This could be considered to be your morals, your opinions, and the culmination of decision points that you both consciously and subconsciously make. This is the real life realization of the analogy of the current course you have set. I implore you to consider the integrity of this. Don't just make changes because a change can be made. Edward Abbey, essayist, and early environmental conservationist said, "Growth for the sake of growth is the ideology of the cancer cell." Integrity is defined as a concept of consistency of actions, values, methods, measures, principles, expectations, and outcomes. In ethics, integrity is regarded as the honesty and truthfulness or accuracy of one's actions. Integrity is a core to our lives.

I experienced the importance of integrity while serving on the submarine. During a maintenance period, a large piece of equipment needed to be serviced; the only way to complete this maintenance was by cutting a large hole in the submarine's hull, the very skin that kept separated the crew from the thousands of pounds of seawater while submerged. Obviously this was performed in port, but was not in dry dock. As a safety precaution, a sailor was to be continuously stationed at the hull cut so that seawater, for any reason, would not be allowed to start filling the engine room.

I was stationed as a hull cut watch several times during the maintenance period, and sat topside, dangling my legs into the engine room. After the maintenance period was over, welders welded the piece of hull back into place; they did all the tests to ensure "water tight integrity" of this procedure, this was a relatively common practice, and the Navy had put all the necessary controls and quality tests in place, but after that hull cut, while submerged, I would always pause in the engine room under where that hull cut had been and look up.

I had been to sea several times before the hull cut, and the water tight integrity of the ship had been proven to me. After the hull cut, my perception of that integrity had been damaged, and it caused quite a bit of consternation with me. I served aboard that submarine for quite a time after the hull cut, and eventually I grew to accept the integrity of that lifesaving hull, but it did take time.

Like the hull cut, you must maintain the integrity of you. Be willing to evolve, be willing to accept change, but always maintain your integrity. The maintenance of your integrity will make create happiness and will aid you in being a part of the social fabric.

In closing, there is a story of where Jesus raised Lazarus from the dead. As Jesus was commencing to resurrect Lazarus, someone said, "He's been dead four days."

Jesus not deterred, continued.

"He stinks"," the person added, yet Jesus continued, and according to the legend, Lazarus was raised from the dead.

No matter who you are, no matter how sure of yourself, no matter what your abilities, and even past accomplishments, there are going to be people around you who will doubt you. And who will try to keep you from accomplishing what you can. You must be sure of yourself, make your decisions, and keep the faith in yourself.

Marvin L. C. Hoffman, a software developer is a founder of Medkinetics, a complete provider data experience for hospitals and private practices. Marvin spent several years in the United States Navy, completing extensive training for the operation of the Navy's fleet of nuclear powered ships. After training, Marvin served on the submarine USS Phoenix for almost four years.

In 1990 two things changed Marvin's life; his first son was born, and he started working at the Oak Ridge National Laboratory. The former was the most life changing, but the latter was where he discovered his talent with computers, and software development.

Marvin enjoys hiking, and sipping his way through coffee and book shops. An avid film-buff, Marvin loves seeing his childhood comic book heroes come to life in movies. Marvin is currently completing a collection of short stories.

Creating a Happy Life

By John Willcocks

There are so many things to fill up your time: films to watch, music to listen to, games to play, books to read. Why should you bother to read what's in this book? It's a good question. To suggest one answer, I'll tell you a very short story; it's a little like a joke, and it's almost funny.

A Story

There was a man, Eric, and most people would consider he was very successful. He had his own business, had a big bank account, and owned a big house, fast car, even a boat. Eric was good at giving orders, telling people what to do to make his business successful. But a dark cloud hung over him: he wasn't happy and it bothered him. He thought there had to be a formula, a method, a secret to happiness.

If there's a secret, he thought, *I can find out what it is.*

So, he went searching for it: the secret to happiness. Because he always wanted everything to be supersized, he went searching for the secret to *eternal* happiness.

Eric travelled the world and everywhere he went he asked people if they knew where he could find the secret to eternal happiness. For years, he travelled the regions of the world until he washed up on the shores of India. He spent a further year wandering around India always asking the same question. Then, one day, in south India a merchant said he knew where he could find what he was looking for. The merchant told him about an old hermit living in a cave at the top of a nearby mountain. Eric set out immediately. He walked day and night for two days, excitement mounting within him, until early one morning he arrived at the top of the mountain and saw the hermit sitting outside his cave watching the sun come up. At his approach, the hermit turned his mild friendly expression upon him.

"I'm told you know the secret to eternal happiness," said Eric. The hermit just nodded. "Will you share it with me?" Again the hermit nodded. There was a long pause. "Well?" said Eric.

The hermit drew a deep breath. "The secret to eternal happiness," he said and, hearing that, Eric's eyes were bright, eager, shining. "The secret to eternal happiness," the hermit repeated.

"Yes, yes..." said Eric, almost dancing up and down with excitement.

"Is..." another pause, "...to agree with everyone you meet."

Eric stopped perfectly still, stunned by what he had just heard. He frowned, and then he shouted furiously, "That isn't the secret to eternal happiness!"

"OK," said the hermit. "It isn't."

I did say it was almost funny. While you are still smiling (I hope) what can we take away from this story? One thing is that happiness (or anything else) is different things for different people. That is fairly obvious. Everyone has different perspectives on life and different isn't wrong, it's just different.

Another thing we might take away is that we are not always ready to hear certain things, accept certain things, or even contemplate certain things. Our guy, Eric, certainly wasn't ready to hear what the hermit said. He didn't want to accept the hermit's view on happiness and he rejected it completely.

The contributors to this book are all regular guys who, many years ago, were standing right where you are today. None of them are telling lies or spinning you a yarn but they are talking about life as they have experienced it and the lessons they have learned. You can accept what you read or you can reject it (not recommended). We would ask that you think about what you read, go one step further than Eric, be smarter than him, talk about some of the things you read with people that are close to you. Who knows, some of these ideas might resonate with you and you'll have the jump on everyone else and be ready for the things life will throw at you?

The Readiness Is All

The title of this section is a quotation from *Hamlet*. Hamlet, the character, spends most of the play trapped by his own uncertainty and indecision about what to do with his situation. But, towards the end of the play, when he says, "The readiness is all," he has come to accept what has happened and is able to move on and take action. The fact he ends up dead doesn't change the fact that he has grown as a person. Anyway, it wouldn't be a tragedy if he ended up happily married with two kids, would it?

What is it that makes us ready to hear something? Well, it's age, the experiences we've had, what culture we come from, and just who we are with our personality, the attitudes we've formed, and a host of other influences. Being ready is, in a sense, being prepared. Being prepared is like laying foundations. If you have good solid foundations, you can expect good results or outcomes.

Here is a practical example. My neighbor and I decided independently of each other to build some raised planters in our yards and we both used the same kind of stone bricks. I dug a trench about 18 inches deep. I then put in the trench a layer of broken bricks and stones, which were about the size of my fist. I followed that by a layer of gravel that filled in the spaces between the bricks and stones. Then I added more gravel a couple inches deep above the bricks and stones. Finally, I poured on a layer of sand to fill in the tiny spaces in the gravel, then a couple more inches of sand. It was hard, hot, thirsty work but a rock solid foundation for my raised planters. I built the walls of the planters, filled them with dirt, and they were ready for the plants. The entire project took me about two months—there were a lot of planters. My neighbor built his planters by laying the stone bricks straight on the ground; he filled them with dirt and they were ready for the plants. The entire project took him about a week.

When we had finished, we surveyed our work and both agreed we had done a good job and both sets of planters looked pretty good. "A good week's work," said my neighbor, which was a little joke on me as I had taken so long. I smiled. It's now six years later and every day I can look out of my kitchen window and see my planters. They look great: clean straight lines, solid construction, the plants have matured and it is a perfect picture; it gives me a lot of pleasure. I can't see my neighbor's planters from my kitchen window but stepping outside gives me a good view. They look a bit like a sand castle that someone has sat on, someone large and heavy. The bricks have sunk into the ground in some places more than others, many of the bricks have cracked, dirt has spilled out, and the entire impression is of a sad dilapidated mess. Good preparation is everything and the readiness is all.

So, how can you be ready for what life throws at you? The truthful answer, of course, is that you can't be ready for everything; but you can do some things to get you in good shape, or be better prepared, for some of life's curve balls. There is a famous quotation often attributed to Benjamin Franklin, which goes: "In this world nothing can be said to be certain, except death and taxes." There are three things you need to pay attention to that will potentially delay the first (death) and make the second (taxes) not something to worry too much about. Those three things are your health, your education, and your finances. If you pay attention to those three things, you will be in excellent shape for those curve balls.

Your health... Look after it.

Factors that affect your health are things like genetics, luck, and lifestyle. The first two you have little to no control over, but the third, lifestyle, you can control to a very large extent. Your lifestyle is largely about the choices you make. Here is a question:

True or False: A supersized burger is *not* a healthy eating choice.

If you answered anything other than true, I would ask you to read up a little on nutrition. But, I think most of us more or less know what is healthy and what is not. That's not to say a burger now and again is going to be harmful; I don't believe it is. However, eating fast food and processed foods day after day for years will eventually catch up with you. It can lead to heart disease and a very strong possibility of Type-2 diabetes with potential loss of vision and lower limb amputations. For me, when I weigh up things like that... "Let's see, on the one hand enjoy burgers, or on the other keep my sight, hmm..." it's really not much of a contest.

Here are a couple of statistics: 24 million people in the United States have diabetes and a quarter of those don't realize they have it. Two of the main risk factors are obesity and physical inactivity. So, if you do nothing else for your health, do these two things: eat healthy and exercise. If you don't know what eating healthy is, find out; there is plenty of information online. The important thing about exercise is that it must be fun. If you do it just because you think you should and it isn't fun, you won't keep it up. So, try different things until you find the right thing for you: play a sport, go running, work out in the gym; but, whatever it is, do something, have fun...and stay healthy.

Your Education...Get One

I don't want to spend too long on this; you've probably heard it a thousand times from dozens of people, including teachers and parents. What are the chances they are all idiots and they are all wrong? Slim. Not having an education doesn't mean you are not smart, doesn't mean you will not be successful. Bill Gates dropped out, right? But, how many Bill Gates are there in this world of seven billion people? If you are hoping to be another Bill Gates, I have to tell you—in all likelihood, you'll be really disappointed. Education will increase your chances of success: the more you learn, the more you earn, which is a snappy little phrase I saw online somewhere. However, the truth is graduates typically earn much more than non-graduates.

Your Finances... Don't Spend It All At Once.

The older you get, the more things it seems come into the picture to compete for your money. Without having some kind of plan or at least an awareness of what you need to do, you'll find your money melting away and you won't even know where it's gone. So, here are a few tips to help secure your financial future.

Know the difference between need and want. Money is so easy to spend; you need to prioritize which things are going to get your hard-earned cash. One thing to help you prioritize is to recognize if a thing is something you need, or something you want. We can think of needs as things that are necessary for our survival. For example, we need air to breathe, food and water, shelter, and to be able to maintain our normal temperature. Take any of those things away and sooner or later we will die; very much sooner if we are talking about a lack of air. A want is something we would like to have but it is not necessary for our survival.

That latest video game is an example of a want. You are not going to die if you don't get online and blow all your friends out of the water.

It isn't always as black and white as that but in general, if you can recognize that something is a real need, it is pretty clear that there is no decision to make, you have to go for it. What is difficult is prioritizing all those wants. One way to do that is to assess what bad things or good things might happen if you did or didn't get that thing you want. Another way is to exercise self-control. Exercise self-control. I wrote it again because it is so much easier to say it or write it than do it. But, if you just wait and you don't buy something on an impulse, often that thing you really must have turns out to be something you don't care about at all.

Don't go into debt. Here is a question for you. You have a credit card and your outstanding balance is $1,000. The interest rate on the card is 15 percent, which is an average rate. Are your eyes glazing over? Has your brain switched off? Stick with it; here is the question. If you pay just the minimum payment of $20 on time each month, how long will it take you to pay off that debt? This is assuming you never use the card again.

A. One year

B. Four years

C. Seven years

If you answered seven years, you were right! Seven years and you can't use the card again AND you have to pay on time or they add penalty charges or late fees. Over seven years, you'll pay nearly $600 in interest. Here is an example of what bad news that is. You see a pair of shoes on sale; they are marked down from $70 to $50. A bargain, you think, so you buy them on your credit card. You wear them for a couple of years, they wear out, and you throw them away. If they were on that card we were talking about in the question, you are still paying for those shoes for five years after you threw them away! Additionally, with the interest charges, you end up paying not $50 for the shoes but $80. That's really not much of a bargain, is it?

Okay, I said don't go into debt; but, of course we all have to go into debt, most of us anyway when we buy a house. We could see that as "good" debt. You can often see your house as an investment as it goes up in value over the time you live in it and you can sell it for more than you paid for it. Don't bank on that, though, as it is not guaranteed. My point is, don't go into debt for a pair of shoes, groceries, or a haircut. That would be bad debt. And, if you do have a credit card don't pay the minimum but pay down the balance each month. If you can't do that, you are spending too much and living a lifestyle you just can't afford. Believe me—if you end up on that path, your life is miserable.

Save for Retirement: Start Early, Start Now.

If you had a list of "advice from this book to ignore," I imagine this would be number one. You probably think: I shouldn't have to think about retirement *now*. And you are right; you shouldn't have to think about where you'll retire or what you'll be doing day to day. You can enjoy considering those things when the time comes. When the time does come to retire, and it *will* come, the range of options you have will be much greater if you have the money to fund the things you want to do. The painless way to do that is to start early, start now. Starting early is relatively painless because of the mysterious way compound interest works. It is just a fact that the earlier you start saving the less money you have to put away to reach your goal. Amazing; the earlier you start, the less it costs you in the long run.

I like statistics. I don't like fiddling with all the numbers and making all the complicated calculations but I love the numbers that come out after all the number crunching. The numbers that come out are often surprising, horrifying, sobering, depressing, but rarely boring...umm...if you're me! The numbers aren't boring if you realize they are about real people like you and me with their own hopes and dreams and concerns. The numbers tell or predict a story. I'll throw just a few numbers at you then tell the story. These numbers come from a 2010 survey released by the Employee Benefit Research Institute.

- 43 percent of Americans have less than $10,000 saved
- Four percent of Americans have enough money stashed away for retirement
- 35 percent of retired Americans rely completely on Social Security
- 80 percent of Americans believe they will not have enough money for retirement

If we just look at those numbers, we can see 16 percent of Americans are living in a fantasyland thinking they will have enough money for retirement when in fact they won't. That aside, remember this is about real people with real lives. What would it be like to just live on Social Security? Let me tell you, you wouldn't like it. The most common phrase to come out of your mouth or cross you mind will be "can't afford it." You will say it for things like vacations and a new car most certainly; you may also say it for cell phone, and cable; and there are plenty of people that have to say it for health care and even fuel for heating. It's a grim picture but you aren't going to be in that situation because you are going to start saving and you are going to start now.

Anywhere you look, any financial expert you ask, will tell you that young people are less likely to save. I am asking you to be one of the smartest people of your generation and start saving now so you can really enjoy life when you are completely grown-up.

There Is No Grown-up

When I was a kid, aunts and uncles would visit and ask, '"What do you want to be when you grow up?"

I had no idea, of course, so I'd say something stupid like, "I want to be older."

They'd think about that, smile, pat me on the head (which I hated), and go back to ignoring me, which was exactly what I wanted. No child wants to be any adult's focus of attention for very long. Years later, one of my college professors scoffed at the notion of being grown up. He wanted nothing to do with the idea because it suggested you were finished growing. Despite being in his 60s he believed he still had things to learn, places to visit, experiences to have, books to read, movies to watch, and so on. That resonated with me and I've lived with that idea ever since. To a child, the idea of being grown up seems boring—and it is. If you think you have no more growing to do, you're wrong and you will become stagnant. So, approach everything an attitude that says, *I have something to learn from this*. This applies whether it is something new or something you have done many times before. Try it, and I almost guarantee you will find something new in it or see it in a different light.

There was a time I studied Aikido. The teacher was a 7th dan black belt and could toss people around like leaves in a tornado. Aikido has a series of forms with countless variations. You start with the first form called *Ikkyo*. Our teacher always returned to this first form, to basics, and there was always something new to learn; even for him, a master of all forms. Our teacher was a master because he knew there is always something else to learn from the fundamentals and, yes, even from his students. Maybe he learned from us how *not* to do something! But hey, knowing what something isn't is a big step towards knowing what something is.

Many times I've heard "life is a work in progress," and I believe it is. None of us are perfect and we don't expect to be. But, we hope we continue to evolve and get better at what we do and who we are along with discovering and experiencing all that new stuff.

Pay attention to the things you value

You need to nurture the things you care about and want to keep in your life, starting with yourself 'by eating healthy, exercising, getting an education, looking after your finances, and so on. However, 'if that's *all* you paid attention to 'you'd become self-absorbed, and that's not good.

Don't take anything for granted. When you do, you stop paying attention. If that happens long enough the thing you took for granted won't be there anymore. We tend to think of family as always there so it is easy to take them for granted. But they are still people and can be hurt by our thoughtlessness.

I can think of five things that for me are key ingredients of a good healthy relationship. The most fundamental is trust; without it, you don't have a relationship. You build trust with two other key ingredients: honesty and respect. You have to find a balance between the last two key ingredients: on the one hand, you need to be there for that person; on the other hand, you need to give that person space.

A relationship is like a wild bird; sounds crazy, but it's true. If you take a bird and put it a cage, you destroy the essence of being that bird—a creature that soars joyfully in an open blue sky. Take away its freedom and flight and you destroy that creature; but, give it freedom to fly and you are giving it life and fulfilling its needs.

Same with a relationship; you want to be with a person because you like or love them. At the beginning of a romantic relationship, it feels like you want to be with that person all the time. But, you have to learn to let go and give them space to grow as an individual. So, whether it's a bird or a friendship, paying attention to something is giving what it needs to survive and to flourish.

Be Kind

The Dalai Lama said, "Be kind whenever possible. It is always possible."

It often costs nothing to be kind and no one seriously complains of too much kindness. We can choose how we behave or respond in a variety of situations. Sometimes choosing a response can be really difficult, especially in situations where someone is being unpleasant towards you. The automatic reaction is often to be unpleasant back but the immediate reaction isn't always the best response. That's how situations can get out of hand.

You've probably heard people say you should count to ten or take a deep breath before responding to something; I think they're right. If you just take a moment you're likely to choose a much better response.

Imagine you are about to go out and meet a friend, you're running a bit late, and your grandfather starts telling a story you've heard many times before. You could:

- Roll your eyes and show signs of impatience or boredom while you listen to the story... again. Immediately cut him off saying, "Sorry, I gotta go," then leave.

- Smile but resentfully grit your teeth while waiting for him to finish the story.

- Gently interrupt saying, "Grandpa, that's a really interesting story and I always enjoy hearing it. But, my friend is waiting for me and I'm a bit late. Could I hear it when I get back?"

Which response would be the most kind? I'm guessing this isn't too difficult to answer. The first and second choices are immediate responses and are rude, disrespectful, and unkind. He is likely to notice that behavior and he's unlikely to feel good about that. Choice three is interesting because outwardly you appear to be kind but you are trapping yourself in a situation by being polite. Additionally, you make yourself feel bad because you resent giving up the time and making yourself late. There is also an element of disrespect towards your grandfather because you are not being honest with him. Choice four is the only kind response and it's win-win. Your grandfather is respected and made to feel good because you show your interest in him; and you get what you need by not being made late. Being kind isn't about pleasing people or telling them what they want to hear. Being kind comes from a genuine desire inside yourself to show kindness to others.

There is a benefit for you in showing kindness to others or to animals. You get the same benefit when you care for or nurture a pet. Many scientific studies have shown that doing those things greatly reduce stress. If you didn't already know, stress kills. Stress is a major factor in many illnesses. A reduction in stress means you get less sick and potentially live longer. So, be kind, live longer.

Putting it all together

I don't have all the answers; not sure anyone does. I just have my perspective. I have told the truth about what I believe. Have I missed out anything important? I expect so; but, I have shared with you what seems important to me.

When all's said and done, life is a gift and we should all make the most of it. We share our lives with family, friends, and lovers: find ways to make their lives better and yours will be so much better as a consequence. Think about the ideas in this book and try some of them; you have nothing to lose and everything to gain. Good luck!

John Willcocks grew up in England and spent his childhood playing sports, learning musical instruments, and reading science fiction and animal stories—think Lost in Space and Jungle Book. He's been an electrical engineer, a teacher, and a designer; and lived in the Far East, the Middle East, and now what seems like the Wild West but is in fact plain old Indianapolis, where he pays attention to his wife and his little dog Rosie.

What I Learned From My Absent Father

Dr. Jim Chambers

The oldest of a large family, I spent most of my childhood in a single-parent home and out from under the influence of my father—at least that's what I originally thought. The truth is, I actually learned a lot from the father that I never knew and the older I became the more valuable these lessons have become to those who take them seriously.

Like most young people in love, my parents started out with dreams of a happy home and a prosperous future. Unfortunately, things didn't work out as planned and my father's love of alcohol and other women eventually destroyed whatever chance they had for a normal family life.

Realizing that things were unlikely to change, my mother made a radical decision to move us from our home in rural Oklahoma to a large Midwestern city where she had a chance to start over. It was not a popular decision at the time, especially among our family and community, but thankfully she had the courage to do what was right for herself and her children. It was here, hundreds of miles away from my father, that I learned some invaluable lessons about what it means to be a father, husband, and a man.

Now before you dismiss these lessons as only for those coming from single-parent homes, keep in mind that many fathers who are physically present are also emotionally, spiritually and relationally absent. They may be good providers, coming home to dinner each night and showing up at all the right events, but they never take the time to teach their sons and grandsons what it means to be successful at manhood. They may not live hundreds of miles away like my father did, but they might as well be a million miles away when it comes to building the kind of deep meaningful relationships that boys need to become healthy, functional men. A colleague of mine once remarked in jest, "The qualifications to be a parent are frighteningly low, but the qualifications to teach a boy to become a man are frighteningly high." He may have been joking at the time, but the truth cuts deep especially in our postmodern culture.

Regardless of your family background, growing up without a father who is fully engaged in the life of the family can be a painful experience. For me, it was more than just the heartache of watching my mother struggle to manage a home and make ends meet; it was also coping with deep personal feelings of loneliness, depression, low self-esteem and a sense of abandonment that haunted me well into young adulthood. Thankfully, with the help of a loving wife and a small group of honest men with similar issues, I was able to translate my personal pain into meaningful lessons that have been passed on to my own son, as well as countless other men who crave the same healing. Although my father has been dead for many years now, here are four lessons on manhood that I wish someone would have taught him when he was still a young man.

Be Faithfull

In a few short months of this writing, my wife Lynette and I will celebrate our 40th year of marriage. It has not been a perfect relationship but that's what you get with two imperfect people. What it has been, is a deeply enriching experience filled with all the joys, sorrows, ups and downs commonly associated with life together on this planet. And, neither of us would trade it for the world.

Now while no one will accuse me of being the world's best husband, the one thing that I have been is faithful to my wife. In spite of all that life has thrown at us, I still love her, cherish her, and intend to be devoted to her alone for the rest of my life. I made that promise in a small church service in front of family and friends nearly forty years ago and I plan to keep it. Again, I'm not trying to project the idea that I'm perfect, just that I'm committed to keeping the promise.

It may surprise you, but the value of being faithful to my wife is something I learned from my unfaithful father. You see, early in their relationship my father violated the promise he made to my mother to be faithful to her alone and it has resulted in pain and heartache for her, our family and even his grandchildren. While it took a lot to work through the issues associated with his unfaithfulness, my mother recovered pretty well. She is a strong woman who made the most of her new start, enjoyed a successful career, was able to remarry and raise eight terrific kids. Even today at the age of 80, she is one of the most active and vibrant women you will ever meet. But in spite of her success in overcoming the hurt, some of her children and grandchildren still wrestle with the emotional and relational fallout associated with his unfaithfulness.

In the context of relationships, faithfulness means to stay the course, to remain true to the ideal, and to never waver from the initial commitment. I know this isn't a popular view given the nature and context of our post-modern culture, but I'm convinced that being faithful is the right thing to do for everyone concerned.

If I could go back in time and give my father some advice while he was still a young married man it would simply be, "Dad, don't do it. What seems like nothing more than a little fun will end up causing indescribable pain for those you love the most. If you are unfaithful to your wife it will break her heart, ruin your marriage, and alienate you from your children and grandchildren for as long as you are alive. Be a real man, Dad. Put down the drinks, leave the partying to others, and go home to your wife who loves and adores you."

Do What You Say

Another lesson learned from my absent father is the importance of keeping your word. Let's face it: few things are more important to a man's character and integrity than doing what he says. Without it he can't be trusted and those who make a habit of breaking promises usually become a detriment to their families, friends, employers, and ultimately themselves.

When I was about ten years old, my father offered to take me hunting if my mother would drop me off at an uncle's farm while on a trip to visit family back in Oklahoma. Even though it was out of her way and would cost gas money we really didn't have, she agreed to go along with the idea.

"It's your father," she said, "and regardless of our relationship, you need to spend time with him so you can get to know him."

It wasn't long after she dropped me off that I realized he wasn't coming. In fact, he never showed up, never called, and never apologized to me or my mother for the inconvenience and disappointment. I found out later from a family member that he never intended to a show up. He had decided to go off drinking with his buddies instead of spending a few hours with his son who had traveled hundreds of miles just to spend some time with him.

Once I realized that he wasn't coming I went to the woods by myself and cried for what seemed like an eternity. I wasn't broken because of the missed opportunity to go hunting, or even the rare chance to spend time with my dad; I was brokenhearted because I suddenly realized the truth of what others had been saying for years: My father was not a man of his word. He would say one thing and do another if it was to his benefit, and he would do it with little or no regard for the feelings of others. Some people blamed it on the drinking, others said it was his lack of education and still others blamed his upbringing. Whatever the reason it was a hard truth to accept but I finally got it.

Human relationships are essentially built on two foundations: trust and respect. If you violate one or both on a regular basis you will have a difficult time building or maintaining healthy relationships even within your own family. When a man repeatedly says one thing and does something else with little regard for the feelings of others, he violates their trust. Once this level of trust is broken it is difficult if not impossible to rebuild it.

The same is true for respect. When a man says he is going to do something and then changes his mind without informing or consulting those most affected, he disrespects them at the deepest level. Since no one wants to be around someone who is constantly untrustworthy and disrespectful, they eventually destroy whatever relationships they have, even family.

Although only a child, I was old enough to recognize how important it is for a man to keep his word and if I could go back and give my dad some advice here is what I would say:

"Listen Dad, if you want to become the man that I know you can be learn to keep your word. If you want people to trust you, do what you say regardless of the personal cost. If you want people to respect you, always consider their needs above your own. I know it's not easy, but if you at least try I will be able to follow your lead and become a man of principle and character as well. If not, I will have to spend years living down your poor reputation in order to provide your grandson with a positive example of what it means to be a man of his word."

Appreciate the Power of Touch

If you don't understand the power of a man's touch then now is a good time to take notes; besides, it is not as difficult as you might think.

First, most of the men I have worked with in counseling and group settings over the years reported having little or no physical touch from their fathers other than disciplinary action. Unfortunately this is not uncommon in our culture and helps explain why so many men have difficulty with emotional and physical intimacy. It also helps explain why so many find it difficult to engage in appropriate physical contact with their sons and daughters as they move from early childhood into their preteens and teens.

According to studies on parent-child bonding, personal touch is the single most important non-verbal means of relating between children and their parents. In fact, the initial physical interaction between parent and child not only influences a wide range developmental factors while the child is small, but also plays a significant role in how they relate to those inside and outside the family once they become adults. And while we typically recognize the importance of a mother's touch, we often dismiss the idea that a father's physical presence and touch is equally significant. This is especially true when it comes to modeling what it means to be a loving and caring role model for the next male generation.

Secondly, like many of the men in my counseling and group sessions, the only memories I have of my father's physical touch are negative and associated with being disciplined when I did something wrong. I'm sure he held and played with me as an infant since most young fathers do, but as far as my personal memory goes he never hugged me when I was sad, kissed me on the cheek to say I love you, patted me on the back to celebrate a victory or wrestled with me in the yard just for fun. After several years of struggling with the issue, I finally concluded that I was simply one of those guys who lacked the capacity to express emotional or physical closeness; it simply wasn't a part of my genetic makeup. I loved my wife, and we seemed to have a healthy physical relationship, but when it came to physical closeness I would become terribly uncomfortable and feel the need to push back which caused her great pain. The same was true with my son and daughter as they began to mature. When they were small children I would hug and play with them like most dads, but as they moved into their middle and high school years I found it more and more difficult to hold or hug them when they needed it. Like a lot of men, I was totally unaware of the potential damage caused by repeating the same destructive cycle as my father of withholding my physical affection.

Fortunately, some of my colleagues invited me to a men's retreat where this was one of the topics of discussion. Although they were unaware of my struggle in this area, it turned out to be incredibly insightful and helpful on a number of levels. Here are three insights that have been invaluable to my continued growth.

First of all, more than sixty percent of the men at the event had the same or similar issues with their fathers that I had with mine. Even guys who grew up with dads at home said they received little or no physical contact with their fathers outside of discipline. I was shocked at the time, but discovered later that many researchers in the field of family counseling believe that problems with emotional and physical intimacy in men is generational and can only be changed when someone in the family breaks the cycle. When I realized that this is a common problem and could be resolved, I wanted to be the one to do this in our family.

Second, because I didn't have the opportunity to watch my parents interact as a normal married couple it was difficult for me to appreciate my wife's need for physical closeness. I began to realize that much of the anxiety over letting my wife get too close was due to the lack of exposure to positive emotion expressed through appropriate touch or closeness from my father.

For example, when first married, my wife felt she had to sit close enough to touch me - in the car, at the movies, attending church or just relaxing with friends she always sat close enough to be in constant contact. When working on the car or out in the yard, she would stand right against me or lay her head over on my shoulder to watch what I was doing. To say it was a bit unnerving is an understatement. If you add 20 or so hugs and kisses per day, and the fact that I kept falling off the bed at night in search of a few inches of free space, you can see my dilemma. Although not opposed to being close to a beautiful woman, I simply grew up in a home where physical contact only occurred when you are on the wrong side of a belt or in a fight with a sibling over the last piece of chicken.

Once I realized that her need to be physically close was a normal part of life from her perspective, and that it met her need to feel safe and secure so far from home, I began to change. It wasn't easy mind you, but over time I was able to relax and become more comfortable with the constant touch and closeness that she, and later our children, really needed from me. Now in an attempt to be transparent, let me also confess that if you ask my wife's opinion on where we are now, she will make a compelling argument that even though I'm not where I should be, I'm certainly not where I used to be. There has been progress.

Finally, without my father's presence in the home, there was simply no opportunity to experience the kind of male bonding that a young man needs to develop a healthy understanding of physical touch or closeness. Researchers in both child and family counseling agree that children who grow up with unmet intimacy needs, such as physical affirmation from a parent, are much more likely to experience damaged emotions and unhealthy thinking than those who have those needs met early in life. The fact that my father was absent during my developmental years certainly had an impact on my understanding of physical closeness, as well as positive emotions such as love, joy, caring and so on. Since I did not see it modeled in our daily life I did not know how important it was to others or how to leverage it in a way that was affirming to my wife and children.

If I had a chance to give my own father some feedback on this issue during my early childhood I would have said, "Listen Dad, I know you are a tough guy and all that, but there is something you need to know. In order for me to grow up with a healthy understanding of what it means to be a sensitive and caring man, I need you to hug me from time-to-time just for the heck of it. Pat me on the back to let me know I'm doing a good job even if it's not that good. Punch me in the arm if you feel like it, and let's watch a movie together while I use you as a pillow. I know this must sound strange given your background, but it would really help me understand just how much you love me and what to do when I have a son of my own."

Never Die Young

My father died March 10, 1972, at the age of forty-two. I had just celebrated my 21st birthday a few weeks earlier and even though we didn't have a close personal relationship, his passing was a crucial event. According to the medical and family reports, he died of lung cancer and possible liver disease, which is not surprising given his many years of tobacco and alcohol use. Since our families rarely kept in touch, we didn't even know he had been ill until the day before the funeral. While I don't remember what was said at the memorial service or graveside, there are a couple of things that continue to speak volumes in terms of what it means for a man to die without knowing his family.

One of the things that I often think about is how young he was at the time. Forty-two is pretty young to leave, especially when you come from a family where most people live well into their nineties. From what I understand he was a very bright, funny, and talented guy, and if he would have cut back on the hard drinking and hard living he would probably still be with us. His cause of his death had a profound impact on me, and I vowed to never make the same mistakes. My family and faith have had the most influence on my lifestyle over the years, but his untimely death is a constant a reminder of how important it is to take care of your physical health so you can take care of those who count on you the most.

Perhaps the saddest part of his dying so young is all the wonderful things he has missed. He wasn't around to attend our wedding, rejoice at the birth of our two beautiful children, or celebrate any of his children and grandchildren's successes. He has never been to our home, watched me teach a class, read my writings, or listened to me play music. He has never read one of my wife's wonderful books, met the grandson who is his namesake or enjoyed a day at the lake with his granddaughter and her family. By leaving so early, he has never seen his great grandchildren smile or taken part in any of the birthdays, anniversaries, holidays, or countless other celebrations that we have enjoyed as a family.

I used to think that being absent from my childhood was his greatest mistake, but forty years after his death I'm convinced that this was just a prelude to all the wonderful things he could have experienced if he had stuck around.

If I had a chance to share my heart with him right now here is what I would say: "Dad, I'm sorry you didn't take better care of yourself. If you had cut back on the destructive habits, worked out a little more and taken your health more seriously you would likely still be here. Who knows, with a few more years and a little effort we might have even developed that father and son relationship that I used to dream about as a kid. It would have been nice to have another guy around to bounce things off of when trying to make the tough decisions. Mom did the best she could, but she's not a guy and didn't understand a lot of the things I was going through.

"One of my greatest regrets, Dad, is that you never got to know my family. My wife Lynette has been the best companion a man could ever hope for and our relationship continues to deepen as we grow older now. She is terrific, Pop, and you would have loved her as much as I do if you had only stuck around long enough to know her.

"Our son Joe has turned out to be a wonderful young man too. Married with two beautiful little girls now, he's a great husband, devoted father, and successful businessman. He loves the outdoors as much as I do, and we spend several weeks each year hunting or fishing together. We have often talked about how great it would be if you were on one of our annual father-son trips, and I know he really misses you even though he never had a chance to meet you in person. You leaving has left a hole in his soul as much as mine.

"I'm also sorry that you never had an opportunity to know your granddaughter, Amanda Christine. She has become a beautiful young woman with a wonderful family of her own. She and her husband have a son who is the joy of our life and they own their own business as well. She reminds me a lot of you when she smiles, and she and her family make a special trip back to Oklahoma every year to visit and often stop by your gravesite just to say, *Hi. I really wish you were still here to spend time with them in person, but that's what happens when a man dies young.*"

Final Thoughts

I'm convinced that most men know enough truth to be successful at life, but few are willing to expend the time and energy it takes to apply what they know. As challenging as it can be at times, I want to be in the second group.

It would have been great to have a dad at home during my formative years to help me sort out all the things that a young man goes through as he matures. It would also be nice to have him around today as our family continues to grow and experience life's blessings. The problem is he has never been an integral part of my life so I'm left with the same two alternatives as other men with absent fathers: become angry and depressed or learn something positive from the experience. The lessons shared above are simply my attempt to extract some positive value from a negative experience and help other men do the same.

Although my father was not the best example of faithfulness, I have tried to learn from his mistakes and remain devoted to my wife. It has been one of the best lessons I could have ever learned. Learning that my father was not a man of his word was a painful lesson too, but it has added incredible value to my personal and professional relationships. Those who live and work with me know they can count on me and that means a lot, especially when things get tough.

Understanding the power of a man's touch was another difficult lesson and continues to be a challenge at times. The good news is that I have a loving wife and family who accept me for who I am while encouraging me to continually grow personally and spiritually. And when it comes to personal health, I'm working hard to eat the right things, exercise regularly, and keep my bad habits in check. Unlike my father, I want to be around as long as possible because you never know what wonderful blessings you're going to experience next.

Dr. Jim Chambers is founder of the Institute for Organizational Leadership, a non-profit consulting firm providing strategic planning, organizational improvement and leadership development for public and private groups. He is a popular conference speaker, workshop facilitator and has taught doctoral and graduate studies for a number of universities in the US and abroad. Dr. Chambers and his wife, Lynette, have been married more than 40 years and enjoy working together to improve the lives of others.

Develop Yourself – Develop Your Career

By Greg Kirkland

If you are fortunate to be reading this book as an undergraduate college student you'll be able to gain the most benefit out of the early part of this chapter, but the rest of it applies to everyone. Simply stated, if you are in college today, you can make sure that you complete your degree, pursue internships to get some real-world experience while still in school, and, hopefully, pursue a higher degree education.

When I was a young man in college it was advantageous in the job market just to hold a bachelor's degree. For some occupations, even holding a two year associates degree set you apart, such as nursing. Today, however, almost all professional positions require a four-year bachelor's degree just to meet entry-level job qualifications. That, obviously, raises the bar quite a bit.

There are exceptions to every rule and you could certainly interject that Bill

Gates, co-founder of Microsoft, America's richest man, never graduated from

college. To give a more recent example, Mark Zuckerberg dropped out of Harvard

to found Facebook and he's a billionaire. Those are exceptions, indeed, and rare

examples of inventing entrepreneurs. My advice to most of the population is to

spend your time in school wisely, earn a good education, and learn a good

foundation to build a career upon. The bachelor's degree is a great place to start.

Not everyone entering college knows what they want to be when they grow

up. Sure, I thought I wanted to study math in school, but when I went to figure

out how that translated to a job after school the best I could come up with was

an engineer or a math professor. Neither was what I intended to be. I put my

math skills to work and studied computers and got a degree in computer

information science, and that has turned out to be a pretty good decision all

these years. I do, however, compare my own career to that of some of my

collegiate peers and I find that those that have been more successful than I have

went back to school to get their master's degree, most notably the Master of

Business Administration (MBA). A few of my computer classmates from college

have gone on to be executive directors and vice presidents in their respective

businesses, as a testament to what an advanced degree can provide.

My school didn't offer advanced degrees and I certainly wanted to get to

work to start earning a living. I got a decent paying job out of school for a couple

of years and then moved on to another company, relocated with them, and relocated again about five years after. I got married and started raising a family. Once kids came along I thought that I had no time to go back to school to get a master's degree. If you are reading this and have been entertaining earning a graduate degree, my advice is to try your best at adding it on directly at the end of your undergraduate degree.

I've got a son entering high school this year and I'm already talking to him about the benefits of the MBA. I want him to have the mindset that college is five to six years and he'll get two degrees, an undergraduate degree, and a graduate degree. Having the master's graduate degree is what gives students coming out of school today a competitive advantage. Now, I just have to figure out how to pay for it all!

Internships

The college internship program is a great way to put something in the experience section of your resume. As you near graduation, with a few months ahead of time, you're going to want to start your job search. I'd say even start a semester ahead of time to let companies know that you are nearing graduation with your degree and with real job experience. That experience is called an Internship.

Internships are more business focused than regular summer jobs. I mean I used to umpire baseball and softball leagues during the summers from high school into the first couple of years of college. But by my junior and senior years of college I was interested in working for companies that might actually hire me when I graduated, or at least, would vouch for me as a reference, that I was a good employee and had a strong work ethic. The primary benefit of the internship is to show that you are reliable and dependable and can do a good job as a promising future employer.

Résumé

I believe that the résumé is just as important as it ever was. It is still a one to two page summary of your education, experience, skills, and awards/certifications. Every job application that I've ever completed, every recruiter or hiring manager that I've ever talked to has asked to see my résumé. Rarely in business is it appropriate to "toot your own horn" or be a braggart. You certainly need to be truthful in your résumé, but it is your best chance to tell people that haven't met you to take a chance on you.

Your résumé by itself isn't going to get you the job. The purpose of the résumé is to get you the interview. I think that is very important to understand. You share your résumé to get noticed, to get an opportunity to talk to someone, either over the phone, or in person about your skills, qualifications, and interests. You have to win the job at the interview.

How your résumé gets used today is certainly different than when I was graduating college. When I was an undergraduate student, in the ancient days before the Internet and email, we had to lookup company names and contacts from the phone book and from business lists in the library. Then, we'd have to print, physically stuff envelopes, affix postage, and mail our résumés out to dozens or even hundreds of businesses to get noticed.

Today those tactics don't work, and thankfully, you don't have to do it that way anymore. Today's job seekers can place their electronic résumés up on public job boards such as Monster, CareerBuilder, Hot Jobs, Dice, and many, many more. Those websites *do* produce job leads, but the best way to find job leads today is networking. I've got more on that coming up.

References

Some companies still ask for three references so that they can fact check that you were employed by the companies you said you were, when you were there, and what you did, as well as verify salary information. Many companies will only validate dates of employment and final pay. That works for me.

You want to pick references that you know will have good things to say about you. I've heard stories about job offers that were derailed by the candidate not taking the time to line up references and hastily jotted down a few names and numbers without checking with them first.

Even with approved references you want to keep in contact with them. I took my own advice today and sent a personal note out to each of my references just to keep in touch. References are used much less than they used to be, but you still want to be prepared and come to the interview with a reference list.

Interviewing

I could write a whole book about Interview, and I may, someday. I write a Job Search blog and have over 80 articles in it where I dole out advice on how to conduct the job search, interviewing skills and techniques, what to say and do, as well as what not to say and what not to do. I have a lot of experience on both sides of the interviewing desk. I feel that one of my key strengths as a manager is identifying and mentoring technical talent through team building. With that being said, I'm not an expert and there are many other people that make a career out of recruiting and interviewing that may have competing views on my interviewing advice.

For a college graduate looking to go out and find their first job or the experienced hire that is in career transition, my advice for the interviewee starts out simply stating – be prepared. Do your homework before the interview and know the company history, its products, and services. It's even nice when you've read the company mission and vision statements and can work those into your discussion. Try to find out the names of the people that will be interviewing you and lookup their company bios from their website or via LinkedIn or Facebook, perhaps. It's good to know their title, how long they've been doing their job, as well as their career progression.

Many people make the mistake of thinking that the Interview is all about them. The purpose of the interview is to win the job, but you need to do so in the context of solving the interviewer's problems. While you will certainly need to have prepared answers to routine questions and have success stories to answer behavioral questions such as, "Tell me about a time when....",," you need to convey your answers about how your skills, interests and desires provide solutions to the challenges that the company faces by creating, or backfilling, the position that you are interviewing for. I can't stress this point strongly enough. The interview is *not* about what you have already done, but how you can help the company you are interviewing for solve *their* problems. I know that is a different perspective. One that you may not have heard before, but I can assure you it is true.

I had a career coach recently that described this process using SOAR stories. SOAR stands for:

Situation   Describe the situation

Obstacles   Describe the obstacles you faced

Actions   List the actions you took

Results   Describe the results you and the benefits to your employer

By being able to spell out how your skill set was used to solve tangible problems, particularly pointing out the outcome, the results, will help the potential employer see how your logic and reasoning will benefit them. It really doesn't matter what you've done for someone else. You need to show the interviewer that you can do the same thing and more to help them.

During the Interview you want to make sure that the interviewer understands your key strengths. This can be accomplished through your stories, or if you haven't been able to interject them in any other way, make sure to state them at the end when you are asked to wrap it up. Remember that you are checking out the potential employer just as much as they are checking you out. You want to make sure it is a good fit for you, not just a paycheck. If you aren't going to be happy there then it isn't going to work out for either of you.

Always have a list of prepared questions. When asked if you have any more questions, *never* end it with, "I think we covered it all," or "I'm good." Ask more about day-to-day responsibilities of the job. Ask about what resources are available to you to conduct the project. Ask what training is available for you to enhance your skills, obtain, or retain your certifications, etc.

A great last question that I learned from my career coach to ask is, "What concerns do you have about my ability to fill this position?"

It works very effectively. Either they have no concerns, in which you've just helped them realize that you are ideal for the position or they are going to have concerns. If you don't ask they fill in the blank with their own assumptions, but if they list something specific that they really need not be worried about you have the opportunity to address the concern. Perhaps their concern is that you've never worked in their industry before. Tell them that you are looking to break into that market and that you have many transferable skills and list a few.

As I said before I could write an entire book on just the Interview process and its nuances, but let's move along to the next section.

Networking

What is networking? I'm not talking about computer networks here, even though I'm an IT person by trade. Networking in the context of career development is about making contacts and nurturing them. For example, when I'm looking for a new job opportunity, I reach out to people that I know that might know someone that can lead to a job. Not often do I meet someone that is directly hiring themselves, the person we call the hiring manager. Instead, what we do is talk to people at companies that we admire, that we'd like to work at ourselves and ask some qualifying questions. How do you like working for XYZ Corporation? Do you have any new initiatives going on where you need help (in your field)? State that you are looking for a new career opportunity and ask them if there is anyone at their company that they'd recommend that you should meet. Most people want to help, so they will say "yes." Then ask them if they can facilitate the introduction. That introduction might be via email or over a cup of coffee.

One of my success stories in networking comes from earning a session with the chief information officer (CIO – top IT person for the company) of a major hospital in the city where I live. I didn't know the person directly. I met someone who introduced me to someone that led to a meeting with the CIO. In contacting the CIO he was quick to point out that they weren't in a hiring mode.

I put the CIO at ease indicating that I was just interested in information, that I was interested in the healthcare industry and how does one go about breaking into IT in healthcare. I asked for 30 minutes of his time and he gave me 90. I was blessed to get this much time of someone at this level in the organization. At the end of the meeting he asked how he could help. I asked him if he could introduce me to some of his peer colleagues around town. He did. *That* is how you do networking!

A great business social media site for networking is called LinkedIn. I use LinkedIn as my electronic, online, interactive resume. I have almost 600 Connections (contacts), over a dozen recommendations (references) and dozens of skill endorsements. What I like best about LinkedIn is searching for companies that I'm interested in and seeing who in my network works there. Then I contact them to try to get an internal referral that helps me get noticed among the hundreds of applications that are posted to their job board. Employers trust their own employees, so getting an internal referral is a great way to make a connection to the recruiting arm of the organization, or if you are lucky, directly to the hiring manager.

Job Search

I've mentioned this a bit already but the Job Search process has changed substantially over the past 20 years. You don't send out hundreds of resumes by mail or go walking door-to-door downtown to find the professional job. You network to meet people. You post your resume on the job boards. You apply online to the company specific job boards. You work with recruiters.

The job search of today is a multi-faceted approach. You want to try several things simultaneously. Here is a big mistake: playing out one job at a time until conclusion. *Don't do that!* You get all excited about a particular company. Friends and family ask how your search is going and you tell them all the details and then, for whatever reason, it doesn't work out. It's depressing. It's exhausting.

Go after multiple leads simultaneously. I say it this way—pursue all options. It's just *way* more productive for your job search when you have several companies that you are talking to. Employers and recruiters like to ask how your search is going. You want to, legitimately, let them know that you are being pursued my several companies and are at various stages of the interview process with them. What this shows them is that other companies are interested. If those companies are interested then so should they.

You want to be in high demand. When I'm in the job search mode I've got my feelers out all over town. I've got recruiters calling. I'm posting to job boards. I'm out Networking to meet new people. I'm interviewing. I'm having meaningful conversations with people every day. I truly believe that mentality reduces the time that it takes to find a job and that means more $$ in your pocket.

Career Coach

I've mentioned a couple of times that I've used a career coach during transition. I've been out of work twice in the past four years and when it happened the first time I was grossly unprepared. I didn't even have a resume, as I'd been working for the same company for over 12 years. It stung, certainly, and it happened at the deepest part of the recession. I had to formulate a plan. My former employer was nice enough to provide me the services of a career coach and with her I developed a resume and a marketing plan.

What's a marketing plan and how do you use one for job search? A marketing plan is a deliberate approach to organizing your search and evaluating your target market. I started out by listing the types of jobs that I'd enjoy. I then wrote out a list of companies that I might like to work for. I then used the Internet, as well as their company database service, to research companies. Of course, I used my network to find people that I know that work for those companies and I began to make contact with those companies, etcetera.

The career coach also provided job search skills courses on Interviewing and networking. I took advantage of those. She provided resource material from her company, a book on many job search topics including what questions to ask, how to prepare cover letters and thank you notes. Soft skills evaluations such as identifying your personality type, personal characteristics and assessing your competencies and showcasing them in your resume and your interview skills.

In short, my career coach provided me with 1-on-1 support and counseling to build back up my confidence in pursuing a new career path and getting my life back on track. I'm very grateful for the services that they have provided, and you'd be advised not to overlook an opportunity to get some help in this area. If you are still in college, then consider your guidance or career placement office as your career coach. They provide a plethora of information to help you find a job.

Mentoring

I've benefitted my entire career from mentoring. Personally I've had a mentor since my first job and I like to mentor younger professionals and help them with their journey, as well. My first job out of college was with a small software development firm. We wrote computer software for banks, and my boss, the president of the company, was my first mentor. His name was Charley. Charley was charismatic and people enjoyed listening to him tell stories. Charley broke off from the corporate world to start his own business in his 30's and I truly believe that I gained an entrepreneurial spirit from having worked for Charley, even if it was only for two years. I do own my own IT consulting business today and feel certain that I owe part of that desire to start my own business to Charley.

Having a mentor that is older than you and has had some success in your field is a great person to know. A few years later I worked in a CPA firm and befriended a senior partner by the name of Vic. Sadly Vic passed away a couple of years ago, but when I was with the firm he'd taken me under his wing and gave me some good advice over the years. He cared about me as a person, as well as my career path. I didn't stay with the firm my whole career, but was there for a long time. Up until his death we'd still meet up for lunch and talk about life. I think that having a healthy mentoring relationship with someone that is not your parents and not your boss, but has something that you can connect with is a special relationship.

The other side of mentoring is being a mentor yourself. I've explained a couple of relationships that have had an impact on my life. I'd certainly like to be remembered for having made a difference in the lives of others. In my career I have mentored younger staff on my team, as well as from other walks of life. Certainly, when you have a team working for you there is an opportunity for you to lead by example and make a favorable impression. I'd take interest in their lives outside of work and their family. I had an understanding and appreciation of their work and their need to take time off of work. I also helped junior staff carve out a career path. I even helped people join organizations that I belonged to or help them along on their path if their interests no longer coincided with my own.

I've been good at networking not only for my own job search but in helping others. I have unemployed friends that I've helped find jobs. I always try to help. I'll introduce people to each other and provide endorsements and recommendations to facilitate meeting. In most cases you'll find that people want to help you and I'm no different. I get a charge out of helping someone else be successful. I hope that you'll find that mentoring and being mentored is a worthwhile process to get involved with.

Be a Lifelong Learner

In closing out this chapter on career development I'd like to share one of my simple philosophies with you: be a lifelong learner. Please don't think that once you've graduated from college, even with an advanced degree, that you've learned everything you need to know in life to be successful. Graduating college and starting a career is just a new chapter in your life. There will be lots of experiences yet to come. Even if you are fortunate to a land a job in your preferred career field there are constant advances to keep up.

Please take my advice and vow to be a lifelong learner. Be open to new ideas: attend workshops, training courses, seminars, webinars, read books, read blogs, newspapers. To be truly successful you need to become an expert in your field and be sought after as an authority in your line of work. Once people come to know you as the authoritative figure in your field, you can most likely be assured of career success. Don't just set out in life to earn a paycheck. Invest in your future by becoming an expert in what you do. Your passion for your occupation will pay for itself and you'll lead a richer and happier life.

Greg Kirkland is a full-time IT Project Manager and a part-time freelance writer. He writes a weekly column for job seekers in the IT industry and has been a contributing author to other technology and project management publications. He is a former IT Director and has spent the majority of his 20+ year IT career in the financial field. Today, he is an IT consultant in the state government sector. In his free time he enjoys camping with the Boy Scouts, coaching softball, playing golf, woodworking, brewing craft beer and being Dad.

My Time Machine

By David S. Hoffman

It's funny how you look back on life and think of what you would do differently had you known then what you know now. I look at the youth today and shake my head saying to myself, "I would not wear my pants like that," or I'd see their tattoos and piercings and think, "How could they do that to that to themselves?"

I remember, when I was much younger, washing my Dodge Charger at a friend's house. We had the music blaring out of my Jensen 6x9s only to hear his dad say "If you could wash that car as fast as that fly by night music is, you'd be done hours ago."

Funny.

I wonder how many adults back then shook their head at me the way I often find myself doing at today's youth. I was thin, tall, and had long, shoulder-length blonde hair. I topped out at 165 pounds. I had just graduated from a Catholic high school that did not allow hair past the collar or any facial hair. So of course I needed long hair and a mustache. By mid-summer I was preparing to head into electronics school. Ugh! Two more years of schooling. At least I took the summer between high school and higher education off from work, learning, and anything productive. Most of my friends did too; summer meant having three months of living before heading back to school again.

Back then, I had no idea where I'd be in 10 or 20 years – didn't care. Heck, all I was really concerned about was getting my car clean and where I was going that night. That's just how it was in the 80s: clean muscle cars, hanging with your friends, and dreading the start of school. Deep down I knew I had to do something with my life. I knew I couldn't work at a restaurant or retail store and get where I wanted to go in life. Where did I want to go? I still do not have that answer. My life is still unfurling before me and I still know there is much more ahead that I must prepare for.

However there seems to be a huge gap between where the youth is today compared to where we were back in the 1980s. I do not see the same enthusiasm in most young men when they think about their futures and the lives they'll lead. To me, it seems as if young men are being dumbed-down or not encouraged to think of their future past the next few weeks. Maybe it's our culture today; we are so distracted with technology and gadgets that it is hard to stay focused on something. I once heard a study that found children today have about a fourteen-minute attention span. Fourteen minutes? That is about how long a TV program lasts before a commercial comes on. Young kids are exposed to so much more information, good or bad, than my generation ever was. Even the speed at which people speak has become faster and shortened to communicate more in less time. Typing has taken on a whole new structure with texting, acronyms, web messaging, and Internet apps. Some may say this is efficiency, but I say it is laziness.

Ancient Typewriters

When I was in my mid-20s, I was already married with a child and had a solid career started. I had graduated from electronics school and landed a job right away. It was a far cry from my dream job, but I knew that I couldn't start at the top. I graduated with a degree in Electronic Engineering, but had to begin working on old IBM typewriters.

Maybe you can remember way back when typewriters had a little ball of letters encircling it. The ball would spin around and create what was typed onto the paper. So crude compared to today's technology – but those are what I started off repairing. Yeah, some electronic job, right?

But I stuck with it, worked hard, got some raises, even a few promotions. I eventually got to work on copy machines, electronic type writers and then in the mid-80s something really started to kick off: the personal computer. I was sent to a computer class and started to learn some basic PC functions and how to perform basic repairs. Back then that was a big deal. The average computer was well over $5,000.

Eventually I got better jobs and ultimately landed where I am today—working in a Fortune 100 company with massive storage systems. I'm still working a lot of hours and still want to get a better job someday. Who knows? Maybe management.

But today's world, your world, is different than what I grew up in. In my job I've noticed that a lot of the mid-20 year-olds haven't even left their parents' house yet, and if they have, it is to go down to a buddies' apartment and play Xbox. I don't have anything against gaming, I play a lot myself, but there seems to be a huge gap in responsibility and drive towards working for what you want and what you want right now.

Maybe the technology is keeping the boys inside playing games, browsing the internet and such, when back in my day the coolest thing to have was a cassette player and those Jensen 6x9s. Don't get me wrong about technology, I and many, many others make our careers in technology, and it has its place in the world. I feel it may have taken some of the ambition from this generation's young men. Many have simply abandoned their dream of being a fireman, policeman, or astronaut.

What do you hear young men saying they want as a career today? Huh? What did I say when I was that age? Crap. I was washing my car and wondering if we were going to the drive-in movies or not that night. Am I a hypocrite? Did I really try as hard as I could back in those two years at a tech school? No. If I could go back in time what would I tell myself and then what would I tell my daughters' boyfriends?

There are two sides to my coin. One side wants to relive those years fixing the things I did, and doing the things I didn't. We all have those thoughts, right? Man, I wish I hadn't done that and man I wish I had done that. The yin and yang of life.

I recently read *Crazy from the Heat* a book by rock singer David Lee Roth of Van Halen. I learned that despite all of Roth's antics, he is smart and has a great philosophy of living life to the fullest—and damn it, he's going to do it. For example, after the Van Halen tours were over, instead of heading off to a resort for some rest and relaxation, Roth went on a trip to the Amazon, to live in the jungle to see and experience things that cannot be done from a car or tour bus— meet locals, try new foods, and encounter many challenges along the way. At one point in his excursion he thought he was going to end up dying from an illness from some bad food or water. He once met a photographer, and after talking with him for some time the photographer realized he was a cool guy. Helmut Newton offered to take photos of Roth for free. Not being prepared, Roth went back to his room and put on a new pair of leather pants that were so tight he couldn't get out of them for hours. The photo was of David Lee Roth chained to a fence. So, this freebie photo, created by a newly-made friend, turned into one of the most iconic posters of that era.

The point I'm trying to get across is this: some people will go after what they want and some people won't. After reading his book I felt as if I have wasted so much of my time away. Worrying about things I've done in the past or what someone might think of me and my choices. This all got me to thinking that maybe I should have asked that hot chick out and I shouldn't have said mean things to my mother. Regrets formed like clouds on the horizon. These regrets can haunt us through our lives and there's nothing you can do to change what's already done, what's already been said. Take a moment and just be honest with yourself: what regrets do you already have and what regrets can you avoid?

I have raised two daughters and I have seen the boyfriends come and go in their lives. Often times I want to strangle them and tell them to get off their butts and get busy. So many of them have no ambition, no goals, no nothing (well, Xbox). Even though I felt like I had more ambition back in my mid / late teens, I know there are things I would do differently and I wish someone had sat down with me and told me what I should or should not do. At least make some recommendations.

What would I tell a young man today after my 50 years of life? What could I possibly say that may make a marked difference in his life? Am I someone that simply shakes his head like my friend's dad and comments on their music? Or am I going to say something that will make him pause and think? If I choose the later, three significant things come to mind. So, in no particular order:

Get Some Brains

I know that sounds cliché, but it is true. The days of supporting yourself—much less a family—simply by working in a factory are gone. Those kinds of jobs just do not exist anymore. A few may, but the majority of people in manufacturing jobs will make low to medium wages and we all know that life is expensive. If you intend on having a girl friend or getting married, having children, or just living comfortably, then you better darn-well get educated. Spend time learning a good trade or get a solid education in a field that has opportunity. If you are a gamer and enjoy gaming for example, learn how to program and create the next *DOOM* game. If you don't have some kind of plan, you will wonder what should you do next - and wondering, my friend, doesn't pay much.

One of my daughter's boyfriends was trying to "find himself" and what to do with his life. He wasn't in college or seeking a higher education and at the time was working at a grocery store. So I decided to be a good father to my potential future son-in-law and pulled him aside one day.

I said something to the effect, "I will help you learn some programming languages if you want to."

He seemed somewhat interested, so I gave him a book to get him started and told him I'd help him along in his self-studies. He politely thanked me and accepted the book. And then he never mentioned the book again or asked me how or where he could learn. I assumed he was reading and maybe struggling with some of the concepts but felt he would eventually ask me something.

Well, as time went on my daughter and this guy broke up and the last I heard he was picking up recycling bins from the homes in nearby neighborhoods. Who knows what happened to the book, but did he just accept it from me to win me over? Did he even try?

Another one of my daughter's boyfriends was working hard, put in the work time, and the guy had a good work ethic. But, to my surprise, he spent much of his earnings on computer games. He shared an apartment with one of his buddies and I found out a lot of his bill were not getting paid. He had borrowed money from my daughter to pay some of his utilities. It is not that he didn't have a job or work hard at it, he just spent it his money on the wrong priorities. After months of dating that relationship ended. Years have since gone by and he still works at the same restaurant. My daughter now looks back on these things and I think she sees what she should be looking for in a guy, or what to not look for.

When I, and almost everyone I knew back those days, were these boys age we were working and going to school. Yeah, it might have been at a Burger King, Kmart or at an auto parts store, but we worked, went to school, and still had time to hang out with our buddies. I may not have washed my car every day, but I had a life full of good friends, a little money, challenges, and lots of fun. I guess that is why God gives us plenty of energy when we are young.

But today, it seems as if those goals of bettering oneself get in the way of hanging out. Why go to school and study for a future if you can live, eat, and sleep in mom and dad's basement for free? What is the incentive? I blame some of this on my generation; we're not making our kids get out and work towards achieving goals. I did make my daughters work. Both of them had to buy their own cars, gasoline, and cell phones. My wife and I did help them pay one half of their insurance, I'm not heartless. I took a lot of heat from my kids: "Dad, Jenny got a new car, her parents bought it for her; it's a new Mustang."

I felt pretty low as my kids were driving a 1992 Ford Escort. But here is what they learned and conveyed to me in their later years. Those kids that were given things did not take care of it. They beat the hell out of their cars. Where my daughter's $600 Ford Escort was being "cared for," because it took many, many nights of working at a local restaurant to pay for that car, her friends weren't learning the real value of what was given to them. Many parents today feel that guilt and give in. I'm telling you, they are not doing their kids any favors. They buy their kids and give them way too much.

Maybe our generation perpetuated this, but I also blame the media and our government for a "you-owe-me" mentality. The government is too quick to provide handouts. Anything a man can give you, a man can take away. So, I have taught my daughters not to rely on someone providing for them. Today, both my daughters have studied hard, graduated college and are working in the fields they chose to work in.

You Are Not Perfect

You will not win at everything you do and you will fail at something you want terribly bad to succeed at. There is little you can do about it. Failing to obtain something you work hard for does not make you a loser; if anything, it makes you stronger and better to try again. When you do get it, you may remember how hard it was to obtain it and hopefully you will appreciate it many times over. Nobody owes you anything and you will probably have to work harder than the guy next to you and will probably get less than he gets.

So get over yourself and simply understand that. You are not the smartest guy here. I work with some pretty smart guys in my field and I am probably just an average guy in the information technology industry. I do not think I am cutting myself short, I am just being realistic. I have seen a coworker do in thirty minutes what would take me two hours or longer to get done. I worked hard during those two hours and I got the same results, but some of my coworkers are just smarter than me. I harbor no ill will towards them; I just understand that there are some people smarter than me. No matter how much I learn there always will be smarter people.

Some in our society tell us we can have anything we want. No, you can't. Unless you win the lottery you probably won't get everything you want. Here's a lesson: what you want now, the things you can't afford, you probably won't want later when you can afford them. Now, that does not mean you should not work towards that new car or specialty item that you have dreamed about, but just understand that it is not simply going to be handed to you. You may even have to sacrifice other things that you really want in order to get it.

Some of your friends and colleagues will get opportunities handed to them while you never even get table crumbs of a similar opportunity. Let's face it: sometimes it is who you know and not what you know. Everyone has had to deal with the boss's son who got the job you wanted after you just spent four years and tens of thousands of dollars for school. It is not fair, but it is the real world.

That kid probably has a cool Corvette and a swinging bachelor pad. He may be educated and may have even been in some of your classes and is truly qualified for that position. But he gets the position simply by who he is and who he knows. It has always been that way and probably always will. Time will tell if daddy's boy will succeed or not—you just stay the course, continue to work hard, and hope your ten-year old car starts after work in order to get you back home. Just remember that nothing is owed to you. Nothing is promised to you. You have to make it happen. No agency, no government, no person can do it for you.

Our founding fathers were very smart when they wrote:

We hold these truths to be self-evident, that all men are created equal, that they are endowed by their Creator with certain unalienable Rights, that among these are Life, Liberty and the pursuit of Happiness.

The key word is pursuit. No one, not even John Hancock, has guaranteed your happiness. You only have the right to go after success, to go after your happiness. My suggestion is for you to pursue a life that makes you excited, makes you feel alive. You may have several ideas of what that means, but trust your gut and follow your heart.

I used to intentionally let my daughters win at a video game only to come back around later and totally outscore them, dominate the game, and eventually beat them. When they would throw a fit, I'd ask, "Do you want me to let you win?

They'd look at me like I had something growing out of my neck.

"No, but..."

I'd just stop them. "Well, you win sometimes and you lose sometimes, that's just how it is"."

I think that stuck with them mostly in their teens and now adulthood. I was not trying to be mean, but if I let them win they will never know what it is like to lose or how to handle it. Because if there is anything I have learned over the years, it is you have to learn how to handle failures. If you can master how to address failing at something then you have won.

Be Respectful.

Be respectful to your parents, teachers, elders, friends, neighbors, dogs, cats, plants, whatever. You will go far in life if people like you. If you are a dick, I'm betting they will not like you as much. It may not be cool to be a nice guy; I mean, hey: nice guys finish last! Uh, I do not think so. Usually the pricks at work or in the gym are shunned by most others around them. You might see some people around them, but who really wants to hang out with a self-centered prick? Some people will think he's cool and it may even look like he's winning the game of life, but as sure as the sun will rise tomorrow I will beat him with respect.

I worked with a guy (we will call him Bob) who belittles everyone he comes in contact with. Bob is an expert in his field, and I in mine. But when I need to work with someone in his department I do not go to Bob first. I choose the woman, let's call her Kim, who is learning and struggling to be the best in the department.

Why would I spend more time getting what I need done when I could go to Bob and have it done in half the time Kim will take? Simple. Because I do not care to work with Bob and I like Kim. She's been kind, engaging in conversation and if I need some help understanding something she takes the time and has the patience to explain it to me without making me feel like a seven-year old that just wet the bed. She gives, and gets, respect.

There have been times when I had to work with Bob and he gets the job done. There have been times when I chose to work with Bob. I don't like Bob's lack of respect and attitude, but I still gave him respect—even if he didn't deserve it. I did not enjoy the experience, even though he got the work done, and I would be hard pressed to share any kudos. But for Kim I went out of my way to send an email to her boss. Told her thank you, and reciprocated the respect she offered.

Respect also means not degrading your friends or family just for fun. Yeah, we all tease, but sometimes it gets taken too far. Today everyone has a cell phone and can record, edit and post on Facebook or YouTube within minutes. What used to be letters in the mail or notes pinned up on school lockers that might be glimpsed before a janitor or teacher took it down is now potentially in front of millions within minutes.

Teasing... heck yeah, that is fun and usually harmless, just expect to get it back from your good buddies. Once I went on a four-day, three-night backpacking trip. I was tasked with making the route and arrangements with the rangers' office and my cousin was tasked with planning our meals. If you've never hiked or packed over several days you know that you'll burn a lot of calories so you need good food.

Our first morning breakfast started with Pop Tarts and water. Lunch was a Snickers bar and water. Finally dinner was freeze-dried hikers' food and water. If you see a pack of hikers' food that says "Feeds Two Adults" do not believe it; a pack of hikers' food for two will feed one hungry man. Twenty years later I still remind my cousin of the Pop Tarts. Whenever he visits I'll get him a few of his favorite flavors. Or if I see a large display of Pop Tarts in the grocery story I will take a photograph and text it to him. This is friendly teasing, of course, and obviously he knows that.

What has become a problem, however, is that many people are focusing on very personal issues and making them public: homosexuality, drugs, pregnancies, and many other issues that hurt people to the core are shared in public with the intent in hurting, not laughing together. Instead of a note on someone's locker, it is on Facebook and Twitter. This has become a big problem over the last several years as we have all heard about the teenage suicides and suicide attempts. Sure, those are extremes instances, but little words can cause big hurt—especially if it is in front of a large audience. And once a comment is made on the Internet it can go viral and be impossible to delete.

Respect others property as well. Do not go bashing in a mail box or knifing someone's car tires. I mean, really? I'm sure that will win over the hearts of everyone. Unless you intend on joining a gang, then by all means, proceed: tear up things that don't belong to you. And we all see how well gangbangers turn out. Most of what I've seen ends up in tragedy.

Respect animals, especially if you want to win the heart of a girl. Most girls love a guy who has a soft spot for our furry friends. I for one have been known to make a furry friend everywhere I go. My wife gets a kick out of me as we travel all over the country and I always end up at some point having my picture taken with man's best friend. I understand that you might be allergic, or you don't like cats, or dogs don't like you, but at least be respectful of them. Being respectful of animals doesn't just mean you hug and kiss on 'em. There's also the respect you show with charging pit bulls, big snakes, and poisonous spiders.

Have you ever wondered who you might encounter each day as you head to work, school, or play? Have you wondered if the guy that was waving you for directions could be the CEO of a company? And remember his son that he gave that great job too? He quit. Now this CEO is looking for someone to fill that role? Were you too busy to help? Disrespectful? Did you just flip him off?

Did you laugh at someone as they were in some kind of distress, maybe not life threatening, but maybe needed help carrying something up some steps? Did you ever stop to think they may just know someone who has an extra ticket to go to the sold-out concert?

I don't think many people realize how many people know other people that may have something of interest to them. We're all connected, in a way, but it's up to you to make the connections. To get something is not why you should be helping others. If you are helping someone only because you are expecting something in return, well, you will probably never get it. That's just bad karma. You should help others because it is the right thing to do and then, just possibly, something good will come back your way.

I once was in a PC training class in Las Vegas, Nevada, back in 1990. A few in our class needed some assistance so a buddy and I jumped over and helped our fellow students. We got to talking to them after class and they told us they worked at Hoover Dam. After a few minutes they extended an offer to take an engineers' tour of the plant. Of course, we accepted and followed them to Hoover Dam. What we got to see were things only engineers, politicians and celebrities got to see. We got to go into the water tubes under the dam and I got to touch a butterfly valve—this was an incredible opportunity.

As a bonus, when we were riding an elevator up, we rode with some of the cast from the movie *Universal Soldier*. They were filming there that day. We got to watch some of the movie making and watched the stunt men repel down the face of Hoover Dam. We weren't looking for something for free—we just offered a little respect towards a class mate.

Say Yes to Everything

A few years ago I met a guy who has a ton of stories like the one I just described. I was talking with this friend one evening at a bar, alongside of my cousin who was looking at a box of Pop Tarts that I brought for him, when my friend told me that he always says yes to every opportunity. He said that he does this because you just never know where that may lead you.

He then proceeded to tell me that if he said yes to something and it wasn't what he thought it was or he didn't like the experience, he can simply no longer continue to do it and walk away. Through this philosophy he has met more celebrities and had more incredible experiences than anyone I know.

Of course this approach does not mean jumping from job to job or saying yes to something dangerous or illegal. This is about saying yes to someone inviting you to a dinner party, or out to see a movie or concert. Yeah, you may not really want to go but if you do not have anything else going on, why not? You could always just leave at an appropriate time. This of course does not mean you quit anything you simple don't like – such as jobs, relationships, and exercise. It means that you're open to possibilities. You respect opportunities as they come.

Handle With Care

When it comes to how a guy should treat girls, there is only one way to handle them—with care. This means physically, verbally, and emotionally. I have been married for nearly 30 years and during that time I have seen what words can do – good and bad. There will be moments when it t is nearly impossible to bite your tongue, but by all means try to stop the hateful words before they leave your mouth. This is part of showing your wife respect.

A man should respect his woman and do what he can to make her life easier. If she's cold, give her your jacket; If she's sick, get a cool rag, find the medicine, do what it takes to help her feel better. The love you give to a woman will be returned one-hundred fold if you do the simplest of things.

Men are fixers and want to fix things, but more often than not, when she comes crying about something in her life, she is really wanting you to listen. As men, we will immediately want to start fixing what is broken, but try as hard as you can to just listen. And it is alright to tell her that you just do not know what to say right now or that you wish there were something you could do. Try to hold hands in public, give her kisses when in an elevator, find that special connection between you two and nurture it. Have fun with her even if it is in the oddest ways.

For example, I had a picture of the demon from the movie *The Exorcist*. It's a scary, horrible-looking creature, but I taped it on the inside of her car's vanity mirror. I imagined her eventually flipping the mirror down and the picture would startle her. Time went by and nothing was ever said, I went and looked for the picture thinking she had not yet found it. But it was gone. Soon afterwards while opening my closet door—*BAM*—there it was – and it scared the crap out of me. This surprise photo exchange went back and forth for months and we had a lot of fun with something simple.

The Edgy Side

While getting a good education and working towards a goal that you may or may not obtain and showing respect are all good things, I have to show a little bit of the other side of the coin. This side of the coin is not meant to be the opposite, but a bit edgier. The three things I have listed above paint the picture of a perfect, clean-cut, young man. But that is not me; I am far from that image I've presented for you to aspire to.

Remember, this is what I would have said to myself if I could jump back into that time machine. But this side of the coin is not dark, nor rusty; this side of the coin is just a bit livelier. The things I am about to mention I do not condone or encourage you to do, but these were part of my life and it is these experiences and hard-learned lessons that has formed me into the man I am today. There are some things I would not have done differently and some I would do again in a heartbeat.

Pot, marijuana, weed; whatever you want to call it today doesn't really matter. Weed was around when I was growing up. Is it ok to smoke pot? Well no, but ahem! I think most of us did it at one time. As a matter of fact I was once at a friend's house and they broke out a joint. I had smoked once or twice before but nothing amazing happened from the pot. But this night when I was passed the doobie, I took a hit and passed it on. While I was still holding my breath I took a big swig of my soda pop and somehow the carbonation caused me to have, the best way I can describe it, a vapor lock in my lungs. I could hardly exhale or breathe in. All my friends were looking at me, making sure I was okay. After a few moments I let out a belch that would make any high school boy proud. But in my case along with it came smoke, I guess still trapped in my lungs. I can still recall my buddies laughing as a ring of heavy pot smoke slowly rose in front of my face.

As the evening came to a close they decided they were going to go get something to eat, I said I was just going to head on home. Good thing for me I passed on that opportunity as my friends ended up in a state penitentiary that night for public intoxication. Today times are different and I am not sure how I feel about pot. So many want it to be legal, but I'm not certain that's really a good thing. It is a mind-altering drug and therefore should not be used while driving, at work, or flying a plane load of people to Florida. My advice to a young man is to stay away from it, but if you do partake, do so as little as possible and only when in a safe environment. If you're going to get high on pot, stay home.

Should you drink and drive? Hell no. But back in my days the cops would just have you pour it out and tell you to go home. The cops might threaten to call your parents if you were really drunk. Today they will lock you up and charge you in court. Because alcohol is legal and readily available, I've had my fair share of alcohol-related events. Back in 1991, shortly after my mother had passed away, my wife and I decided to host a New Year's Eve party at our home. My wife and I invited several couples over for an evening of fun, food, and festivities. As the day progressed, and I was cleaning house while my wife was busy cooking, the phone rang. Answering it, on the other end was one of the couples that were invited telling us they could not make it. As time continued on several more calls came in and eventually everyone had cancelled. That left me and my wife with at least a case of beer, a fifth of whiskey, and all kinds of food and party favors that would not be used. As darkness drew, my wife's aunt and her boyfriend stopped over. They joined us for dinner and we played cards. I was kind of stewing over the fact that my friends had dumped me so I decided to just start eating the food and drinking the drinks. By midnight I had drank about 10 beers and over half of that fifth of whiskey. Needless to say I had a few too many.

To my surprise, after the New Year rang, some of my close friends that were invited decided to come over. At that point I did not care they'd snubbed me, because by now I was loaded on beer and whiskey. I turned up the music, served up drinks for my friends, and began dancing around. Thanks to my martial arts experience I was a pretty flexible guy, but what happened next, well no kung-fu could prepare me for.

While dancing and being silly I jumped about three-feet into the air and did a front to back split in the air. That was all fine and dandy but gravity happened and I landed in that banana-split position. Sounds of tendons, ligaments, and muscle tissue could be heard tearing and popping over the music. I, with a shaking left leg from the injury was able to stand back up, but there was not enough alcohol to cover the pain. I got what I wanted: my friends were laughing, including one friend who laughed so hard that he puked in the kitchen. Fun times.

The next morning I went to an immediate care center for evaluation and was told that I had really injured myself, but they have seen this kind of injury before from ice skaters. Luckily I was prescribed some muscle relaxers and pain killers. The next year for New Year's Eve, everyone showed up I guess expecting an encore. Sorry, not going to happen again.

Most people regret what they didn't do, not what they did (within reason of course). I do not regret those things, I may not do them over again, but I do not regret them. I do regret saying things to my parents that were hurtful. After my mother had passed away those regrets were amplified. I know in my heart that mom forgave me even without me asking for forgiveness, but most people have to ask for that forgiveness. It provides some closure.

I regret a night of drinking and making a fool of myself in front of a girl that I was dating at the time. That night changed her perception of me and has forever changed my life. I do not regret meeting my wife and having my children, just the fact that on that particular night, out drinking with her and some of my friends. My actions changed my life, for better or worse, I will never know.

Lastly, I regret not going after some of the opportunities presented to me. I now follow my friend's advice and say yes when I can. I should have gone with a buddy on a trip to Florida when he wanted to go. I should have gone out with a girl who asked me out, rather than go hang with my buddies after work. I found out this girl had been hurting due to some personal issues and she may have just needed me to be there for her, to listen, to be a friend.

My Advice to You

So, my advice to a young man today is to get out there and explore. Try new things, excel at some, fail at some, but try. Life is about exploration and some day you will be old and someday you will die. How do you want to go out? Do you want to be someone that on their last days wished they had lived their life differently? Don't be afraid of failure; embrace it and move on. This is life and you only get one.

You can live your life to its fullest or just skate by. I skated for much of my life, just being on autopilot. There is no fun in that. Today, I'm trying to catch up and do the things I did not do when I was younger. Yeah, some may call it a midlife crisis, but for me it is not because of an *oh-my-gosh* moment. No, it is because I now realize that there is more to life than I had ever thought of. There are more things to see, things to experience, and people to meet.

Recently, I took a vacation to Yosemite National Park to hike the Panorama Trail. This is an eight-mile strenuous hike down from Glacier Point to the Yosemite Valley floor. On the bus ride up to Glacier Point my wife and I were listening to a conversation behind us. It was a tour guide who was taking Japanese visitors on a tour. The tour guide, my wife, and another elderly lady, named Carol, started talking about the park. I was asking the guide if the Panorama Trail was clearly marked and other hiking technical stuff. I told the guide that we were planning on doing the Panorama Trail and the older woman piped up and said she had wanted to do that trail too. She asked if it would be okay if she could tag along with us.

I had some reservations about the older woman doing the trail too. Could she make it? Would she slow us down? What if she falls and breaks a leg? I decided it'd be okay and gave a Carol a warm greeting and said sure. As we stepped off the bus and began our eight-mile trek down to the valley Carol informed us that she was a retired school teacher. I asked what she used to teach and it was biology and ecology. Wow! Now we had ourselves a nature tour. Carol gave us information about the rock formations, certain trees and wildlife, and things we'd have never encountered had she not been with us. Carol also informed us that she was an avid hiker and well, this older woman, just about out walked me.

There is a line from a Van Halen song that hits this right on the head. The song is titled "A Simple Rhyme." The line is: "I woke up in life to find I almost missed it."

For me that is exactly how I felt when I decided to shut off the auto pilot. I do not want to miss life and everything it has to offer. Are you awake in your life? Are you making the most of everything you can? Are you going to let an older woman hike with you on a trail?

Many people have posted items on Facebook; you know the inspirational posters with catchy wording. I usually do not share those things but I did come across something recently that caught my attention. It goes hand in hand with the Van Halen lyrics. The quote is this: "Life is a journey. It's not to arrive safely in a well preserved body, but to skid in sideways screaming, *Holy crap, what a ride.*"

David S. Hoffman is a systems engineer in Louisville, Kentucky, who has been married for 30 years and has two beautiful daughters. David enjoys running, hiking, cycling, magic, photography, playing computer games, and sharing good times with family and friends. He has completed two half-marathons, Century charity rides and is working towards a full marathon and a half ironman. This is David's first non-fiction work; he has been known to publish a good short story now and then.

Manage Self – Manage Your Money

By Greg Kirkland

I'm getting to that point in my life where I've got a few gray hairs on my head. Heck, who am I kidding? I've got a lot of grey hairs on my head. That blonde hair of my youth is starting to silver. I'm middle aged, yet, I'm at the top of my game for experience, career status, volunteer citizen, community service, husband, and father.

I'm rather fortunate at this stage in the game not to be in debt up to my eyeballs with a home mortgage, two cars, a vacation timeshare and a wife and two kids to feed. Yet, as I look back on my life when I was being educated through the school corporation and later in college, I don't recall *ever* being offered a single class on how to manage my money. I mean, shouldn't there be a 101 – Balancing Your Checkbook or a 202 – Investing in a 401(k)? What about a class on selecting mutual funds? I'm not even talking about risky investments like futures and options. Just the basics of money management would have been a great place to start!

I guess you could say that I took some accounting classes in college. That taught me the difference between a debit and a credit. Maybe that should have been enough to learn how to balance a checkbook. It certainly didn't hurt, but I think all young men and women ought to start out in life on their own with this one pre-requisite: money management.

Managing your money is certainly more than just balancing your checkbook and setting a few dollars back in savings from each paycheck. It's important to plan for your financial future in so many ways. Here's a list to start with: checking, savings, credit cards, debit cards, loans, insurance, 401(k), stocks and bonds, mutual funds, 529 College Choice Plan, IRAs, and I want to touch on the value of your credit report. This list isn't conclusive. Its design is to just cover the basics. If I could go back in time and tell my younger self, fresh out of college, what these things are and how to use them I think I'd be in even better financial shape today.

Let's begin to take a look at each of these financial products, define them, and give some practical advice on how to use them and why.

Get a Checking Account

The most basic of all bank accounts is the lowly checking account. Even if nobody manually writes a check anymore (I know I haven't drafted one in over five years), the money from your paycheck still needs to be deposited into a bank. It gets there through a simple process called direct deposit, which is an automated payment made from your employer to your bank. Almost every employer offers and prefers this method today. Most companies don't want to take the time and expense to print and sign a paper check and the expense to mail it to you or hand deliver it, either. That's certainly old-fashioned.

Utilizing this little service can automatically make you a richer person. Back in the old days of taking your paycheck to a bank to cash it, a lot of people, including my former self, would ask to take some of the money with them in the form of cash. Then, they'd go spend it. I know, a silly concept, but cash in the pocket is too easy to spend. I used to blow $200 on the weekend once I got paid on Friday. Now that the money goes into the bank I have to go out of my way to hit an ATM to get cash. So, I don't blow the $200 on the weekend anymore. I got smart and started paying myself an allowance and do a decent job of sticking to it.

So, your paycheck gets deposited into a checking account. The main purpose of the checking account is to provide a secure source for your electronic payments to pay your monthly bills. I say monthly bills because I'll give you a technique in the next section about how to save money by paying other bills out of your savings account.

Most banks today are sophisticated enough to let you bank online and setup payments to send in your rent, car payment, insurance premiums, etc. It is wise to take advantage of this service. You avoid potential late fees in mailing in a check that misses a deadline due to circumstances beyond your control, such as forgetting, through the United States Postal Service. Automated bill payments will pay your bills just-in-time, meaning it will arrive in time not be late and will be sent as late as possible so that you have that money in your account as long as possible. It's a beautiful thing!

You should only keep enough money in your checking account to pay your bills, cover any debit expenses that you make, plus have a reserve so that you don't overdraft your account. An overdraft is a service charge, normally $25 or higher, for writing a check for more money than you have in your account. That's a very bad thing. Banks are already using your money for free. Don't give them a chance to charge you to let them use your money.

The best kinds of checking accounts are those that don't charge you any money to use their services. Your money should be making you more money, or at least not costing you any money. You don't want to have to pay your bank to let them keep it for you. Banks get paid by loaning money to others and those customers paying interest on their loan. We won't go into that now.

Start a Savings Account

The saving account is, as it suggests, an account for saving money. When I was a younger man, savings accounts used to offer a decent rate of return. That means that I'd get paid interest for keeping my money in the bank. Interest is a fee that the bank pays you for using your money. It's almost unheard of today, unless it is *you* paying *them*.

Let's say the bank offers three percent for retaining a balance of $1,000. That means that over 1 year, in addition to my $1,000 principal, the bank would add another three percent, or $30 in interest. My new balance at the end of year 1 would then be $1,030. That was great when I was a kid. I'd used to save all of my allowance, birthday and Christmas money, work odd jobs so that I could add to my savings account and make money through interest.

I'm sad to report today that banks don't pay full percentage points in interest anymore. We'd be lucky to see a fraction of a percentage point being paid to customers in the form of interest. As I'm checking www.bankrate.com today I see that the national average savings account interest being paid today is 0.11 percent. That's 11 cents on $1000 instead of my prior example of $30. Big difference!

So, folks don't rely as much on savings accounts anymore to increase their riches. Instead, they put aside money in savings just to make sure that they don't spend it in checking. Think of it this way. If you had $100 cash in $10 bills and you put all 10 of them in your wallet. Every time you open your wallet you have a chance to spend all $100. That is what your checking account is. Now take that same $100 cash example and put $60 in your wallet and leave $40 in your desk drawer at home. When you open your wallet you can only spend up to $60. The desk drawer, in this example, is your savings account. You see what I mean? If it isn't in your account you can't spend it. Use that technique to save money!

Here is how we use our savings account. We call it "funds" and we use it to fund (pay for) the larger purchases. "Funds" is used to <u>accumulate</u> money to pay the infrequent items that are billed annually, semi-annually or quarterly. It could also be used to set aside additional money for a future large purchase, such as down payment on a house, car or outright purchase a large flat panel TV.

Monthly bills that you are expecting are easier to keep up with, but when it is time to pay an installment loan or your life insurance or car insurance premiums, etc, you want to have saved a little bit each month so that you don't have the shock of a big check to write when it comes time to make an annual or a semi-annual large lump sum payment.

Take insurance for example. We pay our house insurance once per year and it's a sufficient amount. Had we not set aside a little bit each month and put it in savings, when it came to the end of the year when we needed to write the big check we might not have enough to cover it. I'm afraid a lot of families try to run all of their finances out of one checking account and they don't take the time to plan ahead for these larger purchases and can get themselves into trouble with credit issues. We'll talk about the importance of your credit report at the end of this chapter.

Be Careful With Credit Cards

We Americans love our credit cards, don't we? It's so handy and easy to swipe that card without having to come up with exact change and have the cash in our wallets to cover the expense. I like the convenience myself, but you aren't going to like hearing this. *Don't buy anything that you can't afford to pay for!* It's that simple. It's the biggest advice that I can give a young person coming out of high school about their financial future. Too many young people ruin their credit worthiness by spending way more than their means.

It is sad to see reports that young adults that, along with a college loan, are charging rent, food, books, gas, everything on credit cards with no means to be able repay on a timely basis. My advice is simple. Only charge an item on your credit card if you have enough money in your checking account to pay the bill, *in its entirety*, at the end of the month. No buts about it.

I'll make another similar statement: *cash is better than credit.* It means the same thing – don't buy it if you can't afford to pay for it. A credit card is *not* a loan. It is *not* intended for you, as a consumer, to buy a bunch of stuff and make the minimum monthly payment each month. The credit card companies *want* you do to that. That is how they make billions of dollars. They *hope* you won't pay it off in time and they charge you a whopping interest rate.

I mentioned how great it was to get a three percent interest on savings when I was a kid, well how about you having to pay 18.5 percent interest to your credit card company at the end of the month? That's $185 charge for spending and not repaying $1000. I'm telling you that it is the *worst thing you can do in your financial life is to get upside down on paying off* credit cards.

It is okay to have a credit card. Use it for convenience. Know how much you are spending by keeping tabs on your online account. Pay it off at the end of the month. If you can't pay it off each month then you are buying things that you don't need right now.

Use Caution With Debit Cards

Credit cards were such a hit that someone came out with a great idea to make it even easier to make payments to merchants, the debit card, which is definitely *not* a loan. With a credit card you are given a grace period (usually about 28 days) to make the payment. The debit card is not giving you that grace period to pay back what you have purchased. When you utilize a debit card you are making a *payment directly out of your bank account*, normally your checking account. This is used for convenience, as well, and replaces check writing, for merchants that accept them. The risk is this: emptying your bank account!

I don't use a Debit card. I like to know where I stand with my checking account and knowing that I have enough money in it to cover my monthly bills, as I stated before, and a cushion to prevent overdrafts. If I began to purchase lunch, gas, groceries, and miscellaneous purchases with the money coming directly out of my checking account then I'd have to restructure how I organize my money.

I'm happy with the way that I do things today. Debit cards didn't exist when I was a young man and, therefore, I never got used to using them. Be very careful with them so that you don't run out of money. Plain and simple.

All About Loans

An entire book could be written about how, when and why to use loans, so I won't cover every option in this chapter on money management. The primary thing that I want you to learn is to establish good habits when you are young to buy things only when you can pay for them. Sure, there are lots of things you *want*, such as that new big screen TV, but you need to make sure to take care of your *needs* first. You should only take out a loan to make a purchase on high dollar items that would ordinarily take a long time to payback like college, car, house, or responsible new business venture. I'd try to restrict it to items like that.

You don't want to have to pay hefty interest fees to buy something just because you have to have it. I know we live in the want-it-now generation, but the smart thing to do for your financial future is buy it when you can afford it. Do you see a theme to my advice? It's based on my own experience. I'm not just making this stuff up. I've made mistakes that I hope that my kids won't make and that you won't make either. Please take my advice.

I used to work for a big finance company. We were one of the largest "same as cash" companies in the country. You could finance almost everything from tires, to satellite dishes, to computers and couches with terms like "90 days same as cash." That literally means that you are taking out a loan to purchase an item, let's say a computer, and if you can pay it off completely within 90 days then it is the same as if you'd paid cash up front and there is no interest charge. But, be one day late on your payment and that 91st day comes with a huge penalty. Think 18-25 percent interest charge on that computer purchase. To make it real, that's $180-$250 dollar fee for getting a loan for that $1,000 computer. That's a really expensive mistake and one that I hope you will not make!

Why You Need Insurance

I don't think that anyone starts out on their own in life with enough information about what to do about insurance. Most of you probably first think about car insurance. Your folks, like mine, probably laid a guilt trip on you about how expensive it is for you to drive their cars, or your own car, for that matter. Teens and young adults, usually up to 25, are considered the riskiest drivers on the road. Therefore, if you are in that generation, you, or your parents, have to pay more for the same insurance as someone over 25 years old.

Let's face it. It's illegal to operate a motor vehicle without car insurance, so you have to have it. There are state minimums but having a little more can protect you more against damage that you may cause in an accident, as well as cover the medical expenses of you and the occupants of your vehicle and the other vehicles involved in a crash. It's very important to not only get insurance but to keep up with the payments to keep it in force. My wife's vehicle was hit by an uninsured motorist. It isn't a good situation. Protect yourself and others, get good car insurance!

Outside of my financial advice in this chapter, *please* be a safe driver. I know too many teens involved in crashes, some of them, very unfortunately, fatal. I lost a good friend in high school that was on the golf team with me, and that was well before the days of cell phones and texting. Please hang up and drive; don't be a distracted driver!

Okay, back to the story. Beyond car insurance there is life insurance. I know when I got out of college I wasn't worried about dying and consequently didn't have any life insurance on myself. I wasn't married nor had any dependants, so it wasn't a priority of mine immediately. Within a couple of years out of college a friend of mine from college became an insurance agent and we sat and talked and he helped me become aware of the need to provide for my future responsibilities by purchasing life insurance at a young age. Maybe you are thinking that you need to buy life insurance when you get old so that you can leave some money for your family after you die, and you'd be right, that is the reason you need life insurance. The money management answer is that you need to buy life insurance when you are young is because it costs *a lot less*.

There is such a thing as life expectancy tables that help an insurance sales person determine how much to charge you for premiums. Look at it this way. Essentially you have to pay the same amount for life insurance over your lifetime. You either pay a little bit each year for many years or you pay a whole bunch for fewer years. I like the little bit every year option. It's easier to budget for and one expense that I pay for out of my funds savings account on a semi-annual basis.

Once you rent or own real estate you'll need either renters or home owners Insurance. You have to protect the investment of your property against loss—the more the better. You'll need enough insurance not only to cover your structure but to be able to purchase and replace all of the stuff that you have in it. You want to get back to life the way it was before the tragedy so be prepared with enough insurance. I certainly hope that you never need it.

As I stated at the outset of this section an entire book could be written about Insurance. There is liability insurance, umbrella policies, riders that protect jewelry and things your homeowner's policy doesn't cover. There's earthquake and flood insurance. Even drain insurance in case you have a clogged pipe that backs up water and waste into your home that has to be restored.

Once you get to home ownership, and have dependants of your own, please take the time to check into all of those options. Until then, protect your car, your dwelling, and your own life.

Invest in Investments

Now we are beginning to talk about investments. Investments are things you do with your money to make more money to prepare for your kids' college and your future retirement. If you've been smart with your "money management" to this point, hopefully there is a little bit of your paycheck left over. The wise person doesn't blow this on beer, a new iPhone, and the latest new video game. He sets out to plan for his financial future, a day when he no longer has to work and can enjoy his days in leisure. Those that don't make those plans...well you see them as the greeters at Wal-Mart!

401(k)

401(k) is the tax code for an investment type that many employers offer. The 401(k) is the best investment option that you can make with part of your paycheck. It is a wise investment because money is invested for you directly out of your paycheck, like direct deposit, and it comes out of your paycheck <u>before taxes</u>. That means it is **tax free money** going to work for you. On top of that, many employers will match your contribution, up to a certain dollar amount, giving you further incentive to invest.

Let's say for example that your employer has a matching option at six percent. That means that if you invest up to the first six percent of your paycheck into the 401(k), with each paycheck your employer will also add an additional six percent of company money to that deposit. Of course, you are allowed to invest more of your own money than what the company will match, but my advice is to, at a minimum, make the most out of your company matching option.

To put some numbers to it, if you make $50,000 then six percent of your pay is $3,000. You put in $3,000 and your employer puts in $3,000 for a total investment of $6,000 for that year, tax free. See your tax laws and employers statement about limitations. Nothing is better than free money for retirement.

Stocks and Bonds

I'm not the investing expert, but I acknowledge that part of any successful investor's portfolio is the carefully chosen, selected, and adjusted set of stocks and bonds. Of course I mean investing in the New York Stock Exchange (NYSE) and NASDAQ, the two primary stock trading entities based in the United States. The NYSE contains most publicly traded companies, meaning a company that is owned by its shareholders rather than one or a handful of investors. When you purchase a stock you purchase an ownership share in a company. It's nice to be an owner of a big corporation, but you want to invest in companies that you believe in. You have to do your research on how well the company is doing so that you can try to get a positive return on your investment. You can, and will, have some investments that lose money.

A Bond is a safer investment but not without risk. It is an investment vehicle that normally ensures a steady rate of return. As an investor starts with a more aggressive/risky portfolio, largely based in stocks when they are young, they move to a safer investment mix of bonds to provide more cash like options as they near retirement. That approach helps reduce the likelihood of losing the value of the investment that you need to provide for your retirement.

I, in no way, am providing any investing advice and am not qualified to do so. My advice for this section is to work with a well-respected and experienced financial advisor. Ultimately, the choice to invest is up to you and investments can, and do, lose their value. Investments should be done to make money over a long period of time, such as your working career, to prepare for retirement. The stock market is very volatile and moves up or down every day. No one can predict the movement of a stock or group of stocks and you should consider your investments wisely. Do not try to pick a winner by investing all of your money in only one stock. You would be advised to invest in a portfolio of mixed stocks and bonds.

Mutual Funds

A mixed portfolio of stocks and bonds is known as a mutual fund. This is where I feel more comfortable investing my money. A mutual fund contains an array of investment options and is managed by a single company or person. A track record of how the fund has performed is usually shared as year to date (YTD), one year, three years, five years, ten years and since inception, which means total length of time since the Fund was created.

The successful mutual fund does not move up and down as much as an individual stock or bond. The idea is that while some securities are moving down in one day, others in the same portfolio are moving up. As a whole, we hope that the average movement for the day is up. Over a long period of time, a lot of mutual funds will perform better than any individual item. Even among mutual funds, it is a good idea to have a mixture of funds. My financial advisor recommends, and makes exact recommendations for me, to purchase Funds over a variety of categories and in specific percentages. He may indicate that he wants me to have 20 percent in XYZ Fund, 40 percent in ABC Fund, 20 percent in GHI Fund and the remaining 20 percent in JKL Fund. (Not their real names). Of those, some Funds may be in large company Stocks, some in small company Stocks, others in International companies, etcetera.

Again, you aren't trying to pick a winner with a single fund. Your financial advisor will recommend the right mix of investment products to select for you and your financial goals and needs. You'll likely hear about creating a balanced portfolio or keeping a good mix in your asset allocation. This means that as the performance of your investment products change over time, you'll want to adjust your percentages, and your Fund selection to meet your investment objectives. Again, my disclaimer on investments applies. I'm not a professional investor, nor do I play one on TV.

529 College Choice Plan

The 529 Plan is for investing for your children's college fund. In many states, the 529 Plan allows you to invest money and receive a tax credit for doing so. In our state, we can set aside up to $5,000/yr and receive a $1,000 tax credit, a 20 percent bonus.

The advice that I've received from my Financial Advisor is to setup one account per child. That way, when granddad and grandma give some money to little Timmy for his birthday that money can be put in his 529 Plan that will directly benefit him when it comes time to take money out of there to pay for his college expenses. Obviously, the younger Timmy is when you open the account the longer time he has to earn more money for college. The only catch for this plan is that you'll have to wait until your child is actually born.

Individual Retirement Account (IRA)

IRA is individual retirement account. This investment vehicle is all about *you*. Someday you'd like to stop working, wouldn't you? Well, that day is called retirement and one that we can all look forward to someday. In addition to investing in your 401(k), which is tax free and sometimes company matched, the next best retirement vehicle is to establish and regularly contribute to your IRA.

As of this writing there are two types of IRA's: Traditional and Roth. With the Traditional IRA you put money in tax free now, but when you take money out of it at retirement, that money is taxed at the current tax rate. Many think that rate will be higher than it is today. For those of us that think like that there is another type of IRA called the Roth. What I like about the Roth IRA is that the money that goes in now is taxed now, at hopefully a lower rate than the future, so when I need it at retirement I'll be able to get that money out tax free.

There are restrictions on how much money you can save in an IRA and you should speak with a financial advisor about setting up these accounts and maintaining them, but I can tell you that they are worth while doing. In most IRA's you are picking mutual funds, such as is described above.

Credit Report

A credit report is not an investment vehicle but your rating in its scale indicates your credit worthiness when it comes time to take out a loan. Think of your credit report as your credit reputation. If I was a bank and I was trying to make the decision on whether or not to lend you $35,000 for your new dream car, I'd look at your credit report to determine how likely it is that you are going to pay me back on time, or if at all.

Every time you make a payment on a loan it is reported to one of, or all three, credit bureaus. Those bureaus keep track if you made that payment on time, how much it was, how long it took you to pay back the loan. This is established for every person who ever filled out an application for credit. It includes your credit card payment, your car payment, rent/house payment, department stores, electronics retailers, and all the information about your bills and payment histories.

I don't think that anyone understands the complexity to the formulas that the credit bureaus use to create a credit report score, but I know that they look at the length of good payment history and that increases your score. You don't want to keep open a credit card that you aren't using. This next statement is surprising to most: having an available balance that you *could* use counts against you. Let's say it's a $1,500 credit limit. The reason that it is used against you is that you could go on a shopping spree tomorrow at that store and spend the $1,500. Creditors look at that as a risk in them not getting paid if you go and do that.

It is, therefore, best to maintain the minimum number of loan and revolving credit accounts that you are actively using and require. For example, if you opened a department store credit card because they offered you a 10 percent on a single purchase and you paid that off and never used it again, well, believe it or else, that department card is hurting your credit score. Close it! Having few accounts with a long history of making on-time payments is the best way to increase your score. Start missing payments and you'll see your credit score fall down quickly. Again, it's like your personal reputation. You can lose it quickly, but it takes a long time to earn.

Be very careful with your loans and your credit cards. Pay them off on time every time and you'll build a great credit score. That excellent credit score will be there to help you when you go to purchase your first home or that dream car. Your credit score is the first place that banks and other lending institutions will go to see if you qualify for a loan. Build your credit score. Don't be denied.

Start Your Financial Future Successfully

Start out your young financial life armed with the information that gives you the best opportunity for success. As I mentioned at the outset of this chapter, it'd be great if school would teach you how to manage your money, but unfortunately, most don't. There are probably some schools that do; I'm just saying that it isn't common. Even my parents didn't explain to me the basics that I've just outlined for you. For most, just defining what some of these finance and investment tools are can go a long way towards being educated on doing the right things with your money. Invest and save. Save and invest.

Don't become a victim of this "Gotta have it now!" world we live in. It might seem cool now to have all of the latest gadgets, new car, fancy house, and more, but unless you plan on working the rest of your life, it's best to set aside some of your money from a young age to enjoy your golden years in retirement.

Relationships: Engine Order Telegraph

By Marvin L.C. Hoffman

Relationships can be a tricky thing. For instance you and I, dear reader, are now in a form of a relationship. While I write I have to think of you, the *you* that I have imagined in my head because writing to a laptop screen is just too impersonal. So though you and I have never met, and may never meet, I have come to think of the you in my imagination as a friend; a friend that I wish to share my thoughts on relationships with.

To really make this interesting I will point out that our relationship is one involving time travel; because as you read this, many months, and perhaps years, have passed since I formed these words. Now for the mind-blowing part: real world relationships can be just as hard to grasp and understand as ours. Speaking of amazement at relationships, perhaps we should nail down what a relationship really is before we continue.

A relationship is commonly defined as: The condition by which two or more things are associated, or the connection by which they are related; a kinship by blood or marriage; romantic or sexual involvement; the way in which two or more people act and react around each other; and finally in music the level of affinity of notes, chords, and keys. I told you relationships were mind-blowing; even the definition is somewhat difficult to nail down.

Maybe one of the reasons relationships are so difficult to understand is because they are living vibrant things, often beyond our control. Being living and vibrant, means they change and morph; they grow grander and more elaborate, or perhaps wither and die. When I was seventeen, my father died tragically; his death was one of those *gone in a moment* sort of experiences. After his death, my relationship with my mother changed. I think it was the sudden realization of the tenuousness of life that caused me to be very sensitive to the relationship I had with my mother.

After my father's death, and for some time after, if my mother and I disagreed on anything, I could not leave it unresolved, I would quickly offer up an "I'm sorry" to reconcile any possible rifts in our relationship. My young man's pride may have been hurt, or my silly opinionated self may have felt wrongly done, but neither of those feelings could overcome the feeling of dread looming over me. I had to make it right. So swallowing my pride I would go back to my mother and proffer my forgiveness.

Symbiotic Relationships

It took having children myself to realize that the only one harboring any misgivings was me, in later life I realized that it was me who was the only one holding on to these little tidbits of guilt. I'm still amazed at how convoluted, complicated, and overpowering relationships can be, and can get. And often when you are in a relationship, depending on the depth of the relationship, you and the other person in the relationship will tend to influence each other; you'll get to enjoy the "completing each other's sentences"," you'll find yourself, or the other person, taking an interest in something that you, or he or she, has perhaps not even thought of before. Even the sharing of thoughts and feelings will manifest itself.

This symbiotic relationship, just as with biological symbiotic relationships, is usually beneficial to both organisms. Because of this symbiotic relationship, things that change or affect one person in the relationship will affect the other. It is this relationship between human beings that have formed the intricate societies in which we live.

Some experts think that the inability to develop language skills is one of the reasons the Neanderthal died out. Interesting to consider as the development of mankind to where we are today is pivotal on our early human relationships. And the ability to communicate is no small part of the nurture and care of any sort of relationship. Whether you be coworkers, friends, or lovers the ability to communicate is vital to your relationship.

Sharing between folks is important and not just off-handed sharing, where little or no thought is involved, but rather considered dialog in which someone can know your thoughts, and learn something of you; this is really the glue that helps to hold a relationship together. Without true communication, no relationship can withstand the pressures exerted on it.

I have been in relationships where I've heard my partner say, "You never talk to me."

Usually this is not a literal statement, but rather that she has not heard anything from you that she considers of value. (And usually that means of value to her.) And with this comes the time for careful consideration. If you are tired, or sick, or in some other way not feeling the energy to put into deliberate conversation, you may answer with something like, "Sorry I don't speak stupid"; typically not a good thing to say, but it may be what you are really thinking at that moment.

Like it or not you two are communicating, certainly not in a constructive way, but communicating none-the-less. One of you will have to be the superhero and come to the rescue of the situation, perhaps do some pride swallowing and take this in the proper direction. By the way, if the same person is always the superhero, you may want to consider whether this relationship is actually healthy.

In the "You never talk to me" vein, the lack of conversation may not be the root of the issue. Once my ex-wife and I got into a big argument; and the superficial cause was that I drank too much diet soda. Now my actual

consumption of diet soda was not really the cause of the argument, it was just

the focal point for whatever it was that was bothering her. Something I had done,

or not done, some perceived slight, that may have been justified I might add, was

the real cause, but was also not something that could really be broached. Instead

it was this damned diet soda. This was the vehicle that she could use to initiate a

scintillating conversation. Scintillating conversation equals argument by the way.

This has been many years ago, and I honestly can't remember what my sins were,

but it was not something that led to our divorce, just a pothole on the

relationship autobahn.

Forewarned is Forearmed

Once upon a time I was on the Atkins diet. As far as diets go the Atkins diet

was very effective but that's not my point. My ex-wife's upbringing was one of

limiting meat, and fat intake, so my use of bacon and sausage was very foreign to

her. And there was this one time in particular that I was frying up a large amount

of the meats for my week's meals.

It just so happens that my ex-wife had just had an altercation with her

mother and her sister, both of whom were not present, I might add. My ex-wife

was in a very bad mood, and I recall seeing the look on her face sour as she

brooded on the argument she had had. Unfortunately my cooking meat and I

were in her direct line of sight. The more she would think about her mother and sister, the angrier she'd get. Then she would watch me cook the offending meat, and I could actually watch the storm brewing in her visage.

There's a saying, forewarned is forearmed, but this did not hold true in my case, though I saw her anger mount, and could actually see it shift from the real targets to me and my cooking meats, I could not prevent myself from being sucked into the fight. And yes before long we were in a fight. Even after, I would think back and wonder at how that had happened, like staring at a tsunami until it engulfs you.

Sadly oftentimes relationship issues will 'bleed over' from one relationship to another, maybe, as in my case, someone you are in a relationship with will use you as a sort of proxy for another person he or she is in a relationship with. But even realizing this ahead of time didn't help me, I was still sucked into the fight. I think this is a good time to point out that sometimes, some people just want to fight. Perhaps this is one reason she is an ex-wife.

No matter your opinion of how humans began, our history is brilliant tapestry of these human relations. But without the interrelationships of society, we humans would not have evolved to where we are today. Many archaeologists see the success of human social life as the primary component of modern human development. I like to describe the interrelation of society as a complex web that each and every one of us is a part of. And to be a part of this web is to be connected.

If you research history, you can trace the methods we humans have used to connect with each other. Obviously the basic connection is the physical connection, and this connection allows us to communicate easily; sight, sound, touch, all convey some thought or need. I can imagine that smoke signals would have communicated some necessary information, but maybe to ask if Crawling Lizard is feeling better, another way to keep our relationship on steady ground.

History can show us a lot about people through records such as letters, and these records are wonderful sources to let us know the state of their relationships. You can read the letters of Thomas Jefferson or Lincoln and not just get a glimpse of the personality of the man, but also the state of the relationships they had with the receiver of their letters. Sadly most connections people have are not recorded like letters are. The advent of the telegraph, and subsequently the telephone, were wondrous technological marvels that aided us humans in connecting with our fellow humans.

The computer era has ushered in some great breakthroughs in the ways we connect with each other. Email is one of the most common forms of communication for the modern human being. Technology is advancing at a breathtaking pace, but if we will simply look at where we are today, and where we have been we will see some rather interesting tidbits.

Back in the early days of the Internet, bulletin board sites were commonplace. These budding social sites were places where like-minded people could come together, bond, and form relationships. Then America Online became a big player, yet another way for us to come together. Tracing the growth of the Internet, one starts to see that a very important use of it is in social gathering sites. Places where we can establish, or re-establish, relationships. Chat rooms were a place to collapse that great distance between us and get to know each other. Of course many of these social sites were created specifically for sex, but that, I think, is another essay entirely.

Speaking of chat rooms, it's interesting to note that they are still around, Google+ has "circles," and you can create hang outs. Sound familiar? One of the most famous social sites currently is Facebook, which for me is both a blessing and a curse. The blessing is being able to keep in touch with loved ones like one of my nephews who is currently serving in the Army in Afghanistan. Also a blessing, and I will touch on this more in a moment, is being able to reconnect with past friends whom I thought I had lost in the tides of time.

So what could the curse be? I think it is the impersonal, non-physical connection that the Internet in general and Facebook specifically brings to relationships. I often voice opinions on Facebook that are most likely considered divisive, and perhaps derisive amongst my friends. I will post, or declare publicly, things that I would only share with my closest of friends or family if I were in physical proximity. But on Facebook, the lack of physical connectivity provides some sort of ethereal buffer that makes me feel comfortable making the proclamations.

I actually compare this behavior to that of a drunken man; the alcohol in one's system breaks down inhibitions, and will lead someone to say something that can be hurtful to a relationship. If I were in a room with friends on Facebook, I would most likely not say some of the things that I post while on Facebook. I really need to consider this facet of relationships and not get on my soapbox so much while on Facebook. It's okay to have opinions, but without the direct feedback one gets from being in direct contact with another human being, you can't get the instantaneous sensation that you've said too much, said something too pointed, or in some other way have been obnoxious or bombastic.

You, Me, and Gravity

Like it or not we all need each other. Like cosmic bodies, we all tend to gravitate towards each other. I spent several years in the Navy and a portion of that I served on a submarine. I was part of the crew that operated the nuclear reactor, and my specific specialty was electrician. After some time, I noticed that we electricians would band together against the other engine room operators. But we engine room operators would band together against the "coners" or the other submariners who didn't work in the engine room.

Oh, but I pity anyone who was a "skimmer" meaning sailor on a surface ship because us "bubbleheads" would put them in their place. Yet the skimmers and bubbleheads posed a united front against any other branch of the military. And it was all military service personnel, brothers in arms if you will, together versus the civilians.

Over the years I have seen this same sort of cliquishness manifest in so many different ways. Life onboard the submarine was grueling; long working hours, arduous tasks, and many of those tasks repetitive. I've heard of life on a submarine summarized as weeks of boredom broken by moments of sheer terror. But the cliquishness of our relationships helped us all get through. We didn't realize it but we were forming friendships; friendships forged in a furnace of great pressure and responsibility.

I had friends from that time who were very dear to me; friendships that I felt would last forever. But at that time there was no Internet for us to use, no email addresses, and certainly no Facebook. The best option we had was to get someone's mother's phone number and hope for the best. Needless to say I lost touch with all of my submarine friends. That is until a few years ago, and many of us found each other on Facebook. I can't tell you how happy I was to hook back up with these gentlemen virtually over the ether.

Yet the depth of friendships we had, and having to deal with the loss of that friendship, taught me a valuable lesson. And that was that the relationship wasn't really over. We may not see each other, but I know that I am in other people's hearts just as they are in mine. I may not see them every time I round a corner, but when I sit and reflect on my life, they are there, and just as vibrant as they ever were. It is true now that we occasionally mull over the possibility of a reunion, and it may occur, and I will thoroughly enjoy it, but it is not absolutely necessary.

I believe this sort of relationship bonding is just part of human nature. And because this relationship feature is just a part of our core nature, relationships typically 'just happen'. For instance this social or 'acquaintance' relationship, being a sort of web in which we are all connected is a type of relationship that we can't avoid.

When you go about your life, at your workplace, or in social gatherings, you enter into the wonderful world of social relationships. I'm certain you've used the phrase "he or she and I have a good (or bad) relationship." Maybe at work, you and one of your coworkers, or even worse a superior may have a bad relationship. We adults spend a lot of time at work, and having difficult situations such as this is neither fun nor productive. Sometimes it's just differences in personality, but sometimes it may be something more.

Loving Relationships

Another form of relationship you will most certainly deal with is the close, or love form. This means that two or more people have a connection of care; meaning I do care what happens with you in your life, and I care how my life and my actions affect you. And reciprocally, I want your influence on my life. For me, that's what a relationship means, and this is how true relationships transcend the physical (sexual) level. Many people confuse sex for love; nothing could be further from the truth. Sex is an important part of an intimate relationship, and it's a basic human need, but in and of itself is not the actual relationship. It is true that two people who have sex and nothing else are still in a relationship, and I'm not going to comment that it's a shallow one, or superficial. The sexual relationship is meeting people's needs, and can be healthy and comforting.

Have you ever wondered at the phrase "fall in love"? It seems as if love is something we have no control over, some chemical or biological function built into our brain that, seemingly all on its own, controls our body. You know the feeling; your pulse quickens, your palms may sweat, your mouth may get dry, and all other thoughts go out the window. Such is the power of love. Sounds like a song doesn't it? Oh, more songs have been written over this than anything else. Well, perhaps I should rethink that. Maybe it's when one of the two involved in this involuntary love reaction suddenly *falls* out of love. I stand corrected; it's most probably good love gone bad that has spawned more songs.

I have *fallen* in love more times than I'd like to remember, and I've been on both sides of the falling out of love even as well. It hurts to be hurt, and if you think back on it, you may feel a little hurt of the times that you have been the one to cause the hurt. I do want to make sure one thing is clear; to fall in and out of love is by no means an actual relationship. As a matter of fact, the two are quite often mutually exclusive.

Having an intimate relationship simply for the sake of having a relationship is not a good idea. Like I had mentioned before, relationships are organic, springing from mutual attraction, or need. Not really something you can contrive, just as a tryst with a prostitute can't be considered love, although it can fulfill a need, but I'll not go there.

Dating sites could be an interesting springboard for relationships; I like the idea of a dating site because when you log onto one, everyone there is looking for some sort of relationship, or at least they think that they are. They list their interests; they make bulleted lists of just the type of person they are looking to meet.

I should know: I am one of them.

But I have not taken the obligatory bathroom picture, and certainly haven't done the "duck lips." We, or should I say I, do all of this to try to find our one true relationship. I have known folks who have found love on dating sites, and am hopeful that I may as well. I just find it interesting that we all try to quantify just what it is that we feel will fill that intimate relationship need, when I reality I'm not really sure who it is that will help me to feel truly fulfilled. I can imagine that looking like Jessica Alba wouldn't be a bad start, but that reminds me of a picture I saw once on the internet; imagine a very beautiful woman dressed in a skimpy bikini, and posed very provocatively. The caption stated: "No matter how beautiful she is, no matter how sexy she looks, somewhere there's some guy tired of putting up with her crap."

Jessica is still quite a beauty, but maybe I should look at other things as well. So my strategy now is simply to meet people on dating sites. I have the idea firmly fixed in my mind that it's *friends first*, and perhaps one day I will meet someone; someone who complements me, and I her.

Love and the Lawn Mower

I knew someone who had a relationship with a lawnmower. Now this was no ordinary mower, this was a vintage Cub Cadet; a well-built mower from the sixties. It may have been well built but was not in perfect mowing order though. It seemed that every time he needed to mow his lawn he would have to tinker with the mower for a not insubstantial amount of time.

Now I'm not sure whether it was his cheapness, or his stubbornness to give up a 'perfectly good riding mower' that kept him working on that mower, but I've seen him come near to cussing several times, and for him that was a tremendous stretch. That was always a puzzler for me, I would have donated the mower to a museum and went to Lowes and bought a brand new one, but not him. There was something special going on there that only he had access to, or so I believe.

I think more often than one would like to think human relationships are like this. Perhaps because of personality differences, or differences in political or religious beliefs, relationships are difficult or even impossible to maintain. If the two people are simply dating, or perhaps just acquaintances, then the answer is often simple. Dissolve the relationship. But if this relationship is between work mates, family members, or two married people who can't simply dissolve the relationship then much maintenance, and patience, is going to be required.

I have a truck that I bought for $2500, and I need this truck because I have a popup camper, and I need something to pull the camper with. In 2011, I took a multi-week vacation to Europe. After returning from Europe, I tried to start the truck so that I could buy some much needed groceries, but the truck wouldn't start. Fortunately I know a mechanic who will work on your vehicle at your home, so I gave him a call and scheduled him to fix my truck. This truck is also my only vehicle I might add. After some troubleshooting, the mechanic discovered that a single wire had been severed. He claimed it had been cut, but my conclusion was a little different.

There are a lot of squirrels where I live, and I thought one of them had been chewing on the wiring. But no matter, the mechanic had found the problem, and was commencing to get me back on the road. I had also had him do a tune-up on it, and so I was really excited to get much more efficient ride soon. Alas I was sitting on my sofa when I heard my truck start up in the driveway, so I went outside to enjoy the moment when I heard the mechanic in a panic.

I asked what was wrong, but "Fire! Fire!" was all he could say.

I glanced over and to my horror there were flames coming from the top of the engine. I ran to my garden hose and started paying it out and turned it on. Within moments the fire was out, and the mechanic and I both had to take a breather to get our wits back about us.

Very soon the mechanic had discovered the cause of the fire, there had been a small hole in a fuel line at the back of the engine compartment, so as the engine systems pumped fuel to the fuel injectors, the fuel was squirting onto the rear of the electrical distributor; obviously a tiny spark had ignited the pooling fuel.

When the mechanic switched the engine off, the fuel line stopped squirting fuel, so the flames were just coming from the pooled gasoline. This story does indeed have a point. Initially my repairs would have been a couple of hundred dollars, but after the fire my repair bill was closer to fifteen hundred dollars. During the next year I have had to spend another fifteen hundred dollars on different repairs. So in one year I have spent more than I paid for the vehicle just I repairs.

At what point do I quit spending money on it and just move on to another vehicle? It's the age-old conundrum of which there are numerous 'sayings' such as to not "throw good money after bad." My disdain for car payments, and my need to have a vehicle to pull my camper with, has to be balanced with common sense. And it is like this too with relationships. In discussing that some relationships require more work than others, more maintenance, and sometimes even repairs, when do you say the relationship is more work than it's worth?

I'm sorry to say that I don't have an answer for you. This is where every relationship needs to be weighed and considered carefully. An old troublesome truck is just a tool that I use to get me from point A to point B, albeit sometimes with camper in tow, but cannot be compared to a human being. Sadly there will come a time when you will judge the situation and consider this decision for that human relationship as well. Consider wisely, remembering the symbiotic nature of relationships; ending relationships should not be taken lightly.

Attention, Attention

It should be painfully obvious now that most any relationship you enter into, or rather I should say any relationship beyond the most casual, is going to require attention, and often tender loving care. When you buy a car, a parent may admonish you to 'take care of her', and advise you to change the oil regularly, keep the car clean, and a varied amount of other things. "Take care of the car, and she'll take care of you."

The same attention to detail will keep most healthy relationships going forever. On a nuclear submarine there is a device called the "engine order telegraph" which provides near instantaneous communication of the desired speed from the Officer of the Deck. Interestingly this device uses simple electro-mechanical technology from pre-World War II ships. This simple device let me, as the throttleman know how to spin open or shut the appropriate steam throttle valves to cause the screw to turn and thus speed us through the water to the completion of our mission.

The guy driving the ship, maybe the Captain himself, had a purpose in mind; perhaps some cunning tactic to thwart the plans of our adversary, yet he relied on a simple, almost antiquated, technology to communicate his desires. I still look back at things such as this and smile and shake my head at the humor of this mix of technology. But for it to work, the communication has to be considered, sent, received, and then appropriately acted on.

I can't discuss this in much detail, but there was one time when we were performing some delicate maneuvers where we could not deviate in depth by more than a handful of feet. A submarine 'flies' through water similar to how an airplane flies through the air. The water flowing over the control surfaces allows trained operators to control the depth, pitch, and yaw of a submarine with startling precision.

During these maneuvers I had mentioned, I as the throttleman was ordered to maintain a very constant speed. This order required me to constantly monitor the speed of the ship, and make small adjustments to the throttle positions in order to maintain this speed. I had received the order, and had been admonished through the intercom to more closely monitor the throttles. But I'm ashamed to say that I was not providing the attention to detail that I should have in this. Our speed was fluctuating too much, and thus was causing us to lose some of the precision we needed. Finally, the Captain himself came back and took me to the side and counseled me on the grave importance of what we were doing.

The Captain was someone we all respected, he was the 'old man', and to have him come back and personally admonish me was humiliating. I seem to recall he spoke quietly, but his words carried great weight. From that point forward I paid much greater attention to the throttles, and we finished our maneuvers satisfactorily. No cause for applause here, we did what we were supposed to do. I learned so much from that situation. Though I had been told of the great importance to this, though I had received the communication, I did not take that information and give it the appropriate weight it needed. I can't say that I did everything perfectly after that, but just that one scenario has helped me become the man that I am.

The understanding of that particular relationship, and having reflected on it all these years, helps me to realize how important communication is. But not just the words being bandied back and forth, true communication is the imparting of details or information between both people that cause something to change, or grow between that. At least in the context of relationships this is true.

I, as the throttleman, was in a relationship with the guy driving the boat, and through antiquated technology he and I worked together to complete our missions; to complete our missions safely and to, in my opinion, help to end the cold war. But not only did we have to communicate, one person had to convey valuable information to another, and the person receiving the information had to act on it; had to do something that caused a real change for all involved.

Such is your relationship with anyone. If your significant other says to you, "You never talk to me," maybe he or she really needs to hear something. Sure, an "I love you" will probably help a lot. But be communicative and with that communication be attentive. Perhaps your significant other is not communicating verbally; this is where being attentive is of even greater importance.

If you care for your relationships, be aware of what is going on. In my story of the intricate maneuvers we were doing, I did have some foreknowledge of what we were doing, but I didn't 'feel' the true need until the Captain explained it to me. This lack of attentiveness was most likely my fault, but I think if I were the captain of a submarine and we were going to be doing sensitive maneuvers, I'd pull everyone together and make sure everyone was fully aware of what we were doing.

Good Feelings

If you are feeling vulnerable, or hurt or you feel your relationship with your wife, girlfriend, or good friend it really is your duty to let her or him know. This is being real. Maybe you could say being 'really part' of the relationship. I have written earlier that someone sometimes needs to be the superhero to get the relationship back on the right track. I also mentioned that you need to be aware if you are always the one to be the superhero. But also you need to consider whether you are the one always wearing the tights whether they are needed or not. You are a real person, and you sometimes get sick, you are sometimes confused, and you may not always have *an* answer, let alone the right answer. This is the time to be a real part of the relationship, to let someone be your superhero.

You know that good feeling when you do something good to the other person you are in a relationship with? Imagine how good your partner in this relationship will feel when he or she is able to be your superhero. There are very few exceptions to this with a figurehead such as the captain of a submarine or particularly the platoon leader in *Saving Private Ryan*.

If you watch the movie, there are times when Tom Hanks, being the magnificent actor he is, shows us how he makes decisions and leads his platoon. Yet there is the poignant scene in a demolished French farmhouse where he breaks down and cries. Releasing the terrible pressure he is under. In his position as a figurehead he cannot show indecision, he has to be beyond what would normally be asked of anyone. That is war, and war is hell. This is not a normal 'real life' scenario, and not something that will be asked of you.

My father was not the most attentive of fathers; he was raised in a time when a man doesn't show emotion; when a man had to be the strong silent type. And even though my mind assures me that he must have, I do not recall hearing him tell me he loved me. I don't hold this against my dad; he was doing the best he could; working with what he had to work with. Now perhaps it's the peace and love era of the '70s that I grew up in, but I tell my children all the time that I love them.

I must add that my mother made up for the lack of "I love you" statement. And I did feel loved as a child; I'm not stating anything to the contrary. But the free expression of emotion is a wonderful thing; now I will often get a phone call or text that says, "I love you" from one of my children. And when I hear them say that phrase, or read it read, it is like sweet music to my soul.

Remember the definition of relationship that is musical? Doesn't that make sense now? All of the notes of a chorus united together to make a great music. So much of life is expressed through music; understood through music; and enjoyed through music. Certainly the relationships that I have had, and have now, demonstrate to me that I should do what makes the music sound good. If your relationship with a family member means you need to listen and not necessarily talk, then do that; that will make good music.

I am by no means a perfect human being. I have made so many mistakes, and too many of my relationships have gone to ruin. I have allowed some great people to slip from my life, and I have done and said some irrational or terrible things that have caused relationships to end. This is not something I'm proud of, I don't want those failures as lessons, but I use them as such.

It is by no means an excuse that relationships can be difficult to maintain, cultivate, and understand, but I don't lose hope, nor should you. Remember even the professionals have difficulty with relationships; marriage counselors get divorced, psychologists get counseling, and priests... well, we'll just leave that one be.

Your Life Story

By Joseph Phillips

Halloween 2005

I'm at the Grand Canyon on the North Rim. It's the last day of the year for tourists and the sky is spitting snow. In front of me there's the majestic canyon and I can see the Colorado River like a giant silver snake moving southward. I'm eye-level with the Colorado Plateau and sunlight falls between clouds and dappled red, rocky walls. Jacob's ladder could have happened here; I'm alone and angry so I look for angels to wrestle.

I'm single again, tired of disappointments, exhausted, stewing lost ambitions, and pouting for poor, old Joe. I'd packed on fifty pounds, everything felt tight, I was going bald, teeth ached, and I couldn't sleep. Good food and better wine sustained me between clients and courses, but this life just wasn't fun anymore. And I wondered if this is how life turns out for everyone. Are we supposed to just put up facades and pretend all is well and merely survive? Are we supposed to just look forward to vacations and weekends? This isn't what I wanted. This is misery. Why can't I just have what I want? Why can't my life be the way I imagined?

And then I stood on a boulder and looked a mile into the gash and I thought of jumping, tumbling, and crashing into the rocks below. I thought of ending it all at the end of my world. I thought there'd be no more failure, no more hiding, and no more disappointment. I thought that if I couldn't have the life I wanted then I didn't want one at all. One step and it'd all be over.

My heart beat so fast I could feel it in my ears. Had I really become this low, this miserable? I stood on that boulder for what felt like years and watched the story of my life. Alone, in debt, divorced, furious, all plans askew, and all that I had envisioned for my life jumped into this chasm years ago so why shouldn't I follow? This was my vengeance on life, on God. I had worked hard, I had planned, why couldn't I just have what I wanted? Why are so many other people blessed with good looks, with money, with exciting jobs, and joy? I'll take my life and get it all over with.

And the story plays faster: mother and father singing at the kitchen sink and my brothers playing catch and my dog Samson and apple orchards in Tennessee and Wrigley Field and my son and friends and good things to experience and so much more to see in this life and then I was dizzy.

Good Stories Everywhere

Good stories unfold like new roadmaps. Some people can tell a good story and other people, well, other people just talk. We all have stories. I can make you laugh if I tell you about my brother Sam and the electric fence. Or I can tell you about my childhood dog Samson and how he died in my arms. My life and your life are full of stories. Stories allow us to revisit, rekindle emotions, and share experiences. Stories have a definite beginning, middle, and end.

Life, however, is never so simple. The story of life, mine and yours, is as complex as a snowflake's design and just as fleeting. Is it all random or is it a wonderful story being told by someone else? When you consider all the events that preceded your existence it's incredible you're here at all. Seemingly random actions could nudge a life in one direction or the other: a missed phone call, a lost sock, a few inches to the left or right and it's quite possible you'd be someone else entirely.

Saline Lake, Louisiana, January 1938

A doctor is about to die.

This doctor doesn't know it, but one of the last things he'll do is help my life just a little. He's late for the birth of my mother, arriving just as my mom was making her way into this world. Virginia Ruth is born; she's her parents' only daughter and becomes a sister to four boys. The baby cries and people laugh, shake hands, and excitement fills the tiny house. The doctor confirms the baby is fine and he leaves to go home. And then the car wreck. The dichotomy isn't subtle: the start of one life and the end of another. Miles and minutes apart two families are experiencing joy and grief.

I've wondered about that doctor and his family. Did the doctor have any idea that on his last day he'd deliver a baby? What dreams and aspirations did he have for his children, his life, that were never realized? What happened to his wife and family? Did his family begrudge my grandmother for calling the doctor so late? And what of the driver that hit the doctor? All of these people so quickly changed by the birth of one baby.

Indianapolis, May 1939

If you know anything about May in Indianapolis you'll know it's time for the Indianapolis 500 motor race. There was death here too: Floyd Roberts, the winner of the Indy 500 in 1938, died in lap 109 when he wrecked his car. My grandfather was there and he missed the birth of his son that day. No, he wasn't a fan or gridlocked in traffic – he was working. Too poor to afford a ticket, Grandpa had a job selling newspapers outside the stadium. He never saw one lap of the race, but took the job as an opportunity to provide for the new baby about to enter this world. The son is Donald Eddie and he's the last of six children.

Indianapolis, 1956

Boy meets girl. They flirt. Date for years. And then marry. A few years later, Stephen is born. Then Mark. Then Samuel. And then, finally, I show up. I made it and they could stop having children. Well, except they didn't, as there's one more

boy, Benjamin. Mom tells the story of how they wanted a girl and would have

kept trying, but after five boys they surrendered, recognizing she and Dad were

outnumbered.

If you've been to Sunday school you probably realized that we were all

named after men from the Bible. My family was Baptist; which meant if the

church doors were open, we were there. We went to Sunday morning church,

Sunday night church, and Wednesday night prayer service. We went to Gospel

revivals where fiery preachers pounded on pulpits and wept for our lost souls.

We went to church camp and youth meetings. We were counseled, dunked in

holy water, and saved by Christ's blood. We took our Bibles with us and walked

lopsided if we didn't.

I grew up hearing my mother and father sing while washing dinner dishes:

"Pass me not, O gentle Savior, hear my humble cry..."

"There shall be showers of blessings; this is the promise of love."

We were loved, protected, and sheltered. We had enough, but we certainly

weren't wealthy. There are no silver spoons in my family and we were taught that

it's Christian to be content. Being content is a lesson that's tough to learn when

you're wearing snug bell-bottom jeans that two brothers before you wore.

From Louisiana to the inner streets of Indianapolis, my parents come from a

history of poor families. And poor families create poor families. Mom and Dad

don't tell many stories about their childhood, but they've shared highlights of simple times. Their early years were during World War II: Hitler, Pearl Harbor, and a female workforce as men left for war. My parents saw their brothers return from Europe changed forever by the knowledge of death and war.

Dad has told stories of years when his parents simply had no Christmas. Other years he'd receive some fruit and candy. His best childhood Christmas was when he received a wooden block shaped to look like a racecar and a cardboard dollhouse. He loved them both as he didn't have many toys. As a little guy he collected tin cans, saved pennies, and eventually bought all the pieces to build his own bike.

Mom has similar stories of her family celebrating the entire family's birthdays at once with a cake. Being the only girl, her clothes had to last longer than her brothers' clothes; no sisters meant no hand-me-downs. She's told us of how she longed for a pair of shoes for walking to school. My parents learned to do without, to make do, and to still be happy.

Arizona, 2005

I realized my life isn't just mine to take. My life contributes to the life of my son, the life of my brothers, my friends, my parents, the people in my classes, and the strangers that read my books. And I thought of the grief one step could give my parents, the misery I'd give my son, and the sadness, shame, and disappointment for my brothers. I thought of the stranger that might find my broken body that day or later that year. I instantly realized that it's not just my life, it's a life that so many before have given.

And so I backed away from the edge. The sky didn't part and the hand of God didn't come down and pat me on the head. I didn't hear "Ode to Joy" in the background. There was no fanfare in that moment, but something magical had happened. I realized something powerful and I'm going to share it with you: We can start our lives over any time we want. You can't erase the past, but you can create your future. You cannot control what others do, say, think, or believe, you can control your thoughts, your actions. Control what you can control.

With that epiphany I began to create goals, simple goals, to get more of what I wanted into and out of my life. I created goals to lose weight, to have fun, to embrace joy in lieu of pleasure, to find work that's worthy of my time, and to find a way to contribute to the life stories of others. And over the next few months the shell of disappointment eased off me. I made time to deal with my life and what my life meant to others.

The Absence of Knowing

My parents worked to make certain that we could have the things they didn't. We weren't spoiled, or wealthy, but we rarely went without. We were taught that it's wrong to waste, wrong to throw out things that someone else could use, and wrong to want what others have. If you wanted something special, you had to earn it. When you work hard, save, and savor the hope, it's meaningful when you finally receive it. There's joy in the anticipation, the work to receive something, and the knowledge that you've made it happen.

We grew up in a small Indiana town and had the usual Midwestern life: 4H fairs, sports on Friday nights, autumn bonfires, and radios tuned to Mellencamp, Springsteen, and Zeppelin. One by one my brothers Steve, Mark, and Sam went off to college, careers, and marriage. Now it was just me and Ben. And then my parents moved us to Knoxville, Tennessee. As a typical teenager, I was not happy with this decision. I fumed, felt sick, and longed for my Indiana friends. If ever there was a time I experienced misery it was the first few months in Tennessee.

What I later learned was that my parents were financially on the brink of collapse. A sagging economy, an Indiana manufacturing town where layoffs were rampant, and years of rising interest rates forced Dad to take a job, any job, somewhere else. I had no idea and, of course, they weren't going to confide in a sixteen-year-old the anxiety they felt. I was furious, sad, and lonely, but over time my temper faded and East Tennessee welcomed me.

I drove my old Buick down Broadway and south to Norris Lake. I'd crank the windows down and the radio up and let the wind, summer, and sunshine whip my hair and push me faster and faster. I cruised past apple orchards, concrete bridges, and over a massive dam. I hiked through the Appalachians, saw deer, bears, and skunks. I tried my first beer and last cigarette. I made friends and made it through a final year of high school. And then, a year or so later, I traded down-home Tennessee for downtown Chicago.

Chicago was expensive and this meant I had to work. A lot. There was tuition, books, rent, food, and utilities, but I'd learned lessons on how to get by and got by. I loved Chicago: the massive buildings, the freshwater ocean, Lakeshore Drive, restaurants, and the energy the city gave and took. Every day I rode the El train from Addison to Adams. Can't you imagine? For years the highlight of my year was a county fair and now I'm walking in the shadow of skyscrapers. I could see priceless works of art any day of the week. And I'm living in my own, tiny apartment just blocks from Wrigley Field. How could life get any sweeter?

I fell in love. We married. We had a baby. We divorced. In a matter of months love evaporated, things were said, discovered, hearts and promises broken. The woman I married was not the woman I divorced. And now my life has changed again.

I was going to school to learn how to be a writer, a real writer. Not some hack that cranks out technical manuals, but novels and plays. I envisioned myself as the Hemingway of Chicagoland – or at least a young Studs Terkel. But nope. I made choices and choices have consequences – reap what you sow and all those Bible lessons, right? I couldn't write, couldn't focus, and had a tiny baby to consider. How would I be a dad? How could I be a dad? Am I dreaming? Is this baby even real? But there he is: fat, little legs, slobbery smiles, big almond eyes, and happiness to see you.

So I did what I thought was right: I left Chicago for somewhere more stable, more conducive for a young, divorced man with a baby: Indianapolis. Indianapolis, just down the road from where I grew up was as close to home as I could imagine. I knew people here and people could help me cope and help change diapers. So I sucked it up, pressed on regardless, and worked as much as possible.

Constant work was a perfect way to hide from the pain, misery, despair, and self-defeat I was experiencing. So I made a great income and spent it all. I bought a house, a new car, fancy watches, and vacations. I gambled, ate at the finest restaurants, drank wine older than me, and tried to experience all that I could to compensate for all that I'd missed. I was an expert at feeling sorry for myself and easing the pain with every hedonistic opportunity I could find. And this is how I lived for one long, blurry decade.

Then I went to the Grand Canyon.

Your Stories

I found ways to be a better influence for my son. I found ways to get involved. I studied philosophy, spiritualism, and practiced meditation. I discovered that I wanted to experience all that life has to offer, develop good friendships, and love my family. I am just part of life, just part of a story. Since that Halloween, opportunity has asked me to share my story. I've been fortunate to share my life story with people throughout the United States, in Belgium, France, Germany, the Netherlands, and Italy.

And now, perhaps most importantly, I've shared it with you. Examine your history, your life. How have your parents struggled? What hopes and ambitions did they lie down to pick you up? What things have you gladly set aside to love another? What are you willing to give?

The story of life isn't based on just one character; it's an epic with thousands of characters each taking and contributing to many purposes. Each of us is connected, somehow, to the other. And what happens in your life, in my life, in your neighbors' lives eventually affects us all. All of the people that have come before us have given us this opportunity to live, to excel, to have joy. So what's your purpose? What things will you achieve? Who will you love?

Life has heartache, disappointment, and pain. It is never going to be perfect. There will always be something that aches a little, faucets will leak, things will break, and tears will come. People will die and you'll go on living until one day, someday, you'll reach the end of your story too.

Between now and that future, seize all that you can: Love your parents. Love your family. Sit in the sunshine and feel the grass. Read books to children. Give your best even if it's not good enough. Keep your word. Be alone and listen. Run while you still can. Stargaze. Hold hands. Kiss and feel your heart beat. Find someone to love and love them with all your heart. Have babies and grandbabies. Be the kind stranger. Tell stories and let your stories become their stories.

Joseph Phillips teaches project management, business analysis, and goal setting for organizations around the world. He has taught for Columbia College, University of Chicago, and Ball State University. Phillips has contributed as an author or editor to more than 35 books on technology, careers, and project management. When not writing, teaching, or

consulting, Phillips can be found behind a camera or training for his next

marathon.